British Intellig

The Final Reports

IRISH NARRATIVES

IRISH NARRATIVES

Series edited by David Fitzpatrick

Personal narratives of past lives are essential for understanding any field of history. They provide unrivalled insight into the day-to-day consequences of political, social, economic or cultural relationships. Memoirs, diaries and personal letters, whether by public figures or obscure witnesses of historical events, will often captivate the general reader as well as engrossing the specialist. Yet the vast majority of such narratives are preserved only among the manuscripts or rarities in libraries and archives scattered over the globe. The aim of this series of brief yet scholarly editions is to make available a wide range of narratives concerning Ireland and the Irish over the last four centuries. All documents, or sets of documents, are edited and introduced by specialist scholars, who guide the reader through the world in which the text was created.

David Fitzpatrick teaches history at Trinity College, Dublin. His books include *Politics and Irish Life, 1913–1921* (1977, reissued 1998), *Oceans of Consolation: Personal Accounts of Irish Migration to Australia* (1995) and *The Two Irelands, 1912–1939* (1998).

British Intelligence in Ireland, 1920–21
The Final Reports

Edited by
Peter Hart

CORK UNIVERSITY PRESS

First published in 2002 by
Cork University Press
Cork
Ireland

1 3 5 7 9 10 8 6 4 2

British Library Cataloguing in Publication Data
A CIP catalogue record for this book is available from the British Library.
ISBN 978 1 85918 201 7

Reprinted in 2003, 2011, 2015

Typesetting by Red Barn Publishing, Skeagh, Skibbereen, Co. Cork

Printed and bound in Great Britain by
CPI Group (UK) Ltd, Croydon, CR0 4YY

www.corkuniversitypress.com

Cover image of Sir Ormonde de L'Épée Winter reproduced from *Winter's Tale*
by Sir Ormonde Winter (London: Richards Press, 1955).

Contents

Acknowledgements

I am grateful to the Imperial War Museum and the Public Record Office for their permission to reproduce documents under their care. Robin Whitaker read the text with her usual discernment and reassured me it did make sense after all. Neil Kennedy helped maintain my interest in the by-ways of British intelligence. Further thanks go to Paul Bew and Patrick Maume for supplying missing pieces of the puzzle. I am most thankful for the patience David Fitzpatrick displayed as editor. I would never have been able to finish this work without the extraordinary help given me over the last few years by doctors and nurses in St. John's, Toronto, and Belfast, especially those connected with the Toronto Hospital Transplant Centre and Medical Day Unit, and the Belvoir Park Hospital. To name but a few: Michael Callender, Barry Clements, Janet Dancey, Denise Deasy, Lorenza Durian, Barbara Fair, Mary Flaherty, Ralph George, Paul Greig, Russell Houston, Atul Humar, Vimla Jerath, Les Lilly, Christine McBean, S. Bharati Reddy, Frances Shepherd, Mary Watson, Richard Wilson and Stephanie Wilson. This book is dedicated to my nephew, Peter Hsim Lok Hart Yang.

Introduction

> Legends naturally surround all 'secret service'; its very name
> inspires fear and distrust and stimulates men's imagination...
> Lewis Namier[1]

On 11 July 1921, the Irish war of independence (begun at some inde-
terminate point after 1916) ended with a truce between British forces
and the Irish Republican Army. Opinions were, and are, mixed as to
which side had the upper hand. Whoever can be said to have won the
struggle, however, the verdict is nearly unanimous that British intelligence were patent and inglorious losers. Indeed, 'British intelligence'—out-witted and out-spied—emerges from most accounts of
the revolution as a contradiction in terms: a disastrous compound of
misdirection, malice and ignorance. In the Great War, His Majesty's
secret services had triumphed over their German adversaries to great
acclaim. This time, it was the revolutionaries who were the Kims,
Hannays and Drummonds, led by Michael Collins as the Scarlet Pim-
pernel, while the defenders of the realm were reduced to the role of
bumbling pursuers.

The standard narrative, repeated many times, is as follows. In early
1918, Collins—a rising young leader in both the Irish Volunteers and the
clandestine Irish Republican Brotherhood—came to the conclusion (or
revelation) that the key to revolutionary victory was intelligence. If the
British government and its Irish administration in Dublin Castle could be
denied their usual inside information (supplied by spies, informers and
police surveillance), the revolutionaries could avoid capture and defeat.
At about the same time he was presented with a unique opportunity. A
detective in the Dublin Metropolitan Police tipped him off about planned
mass arrests, and he was (just) able to escape the dragnet.

From this fortuitous beginning, the soon-to-be Director of Intelligence of the IRA (a fusion of the IRB and the Volunteers) wove an
extraordinary network of agents inside the police and civil service,
giving him a priceless advantage in the ensuing underground war. He

also went on the offensive. Gunmen under his personal control—the 'squad'—began to assassinate his pursuers in the DMP detective branch, 'G' Division, in July 1919. Other agents and enemies became targets as they appeared. Collins's culminating masterstroke came on 21 November, 1920—'Bloody Sunday'. This simultaneous execution of a dozen suspected British intelligence officers crippled the government's attempt to recover its position. In a parallel guerrilla campaign, the Royal Irish Constabulary (RIC) also came under withering boycott and attack, depriving the Dublin Castle administration of its 'eyes and ears' in the rest of the country and leaving the IRA in control. By 1921, fighting blind, the British could not hope to win on their chosen terms.

This version of affairs dates from the events themselves and is almost universally shared.[2] Differing emphases have produced two schools of interpretation, however. The first accords the victory to Irish patriotism, daring and cleverness as personified by Collins, an organizational genius and the inspirational hero of the resistance. Nearly all of his biographers—still our main source of information on IRA intelligence—embrace this image. Tim Pat Coogan, for example, calls him 'the founder of modern guerrilla warfare, the first freedom fighter'.[3]

Without necessarily contradicting this view, a second school of historians has preferred to look within the British government and its Irish agencies to explain the defeat. Whereas the first was naturally propagated by partisans of Collins and the revolution (although even the British press wrote admiringly of Irish exploits), the second was originally put forward by conservative and unionist critics of the Liberal and Lloyd George governments. These were the guilty men who 'lost' Ireland through their incompetence and betrayed its loyalists and policemen for their own political ends. More recent historians of Dublin Castle's demise have lost this enmity but have accorded official efforts the same disrespect. As previously classified documents have become available they have revealed a vast accumulation of frustration, error and confusion within the administration and its police forces, and also within the British cabinet and army, as the revolution escalated. Intelligence failure was symptomatic of a wider collapse.

Echoing this judgement, the ever-growing general literature on British intelligence routinely depicts the Irish experience as 'one of almost constant failure'.[4]

Was British failure so complete or so uniform? Was the IRA that good? What did the British intelligencers themselves think? Think they certainly did, jokes about military intelligence notwithstanding. The 1921 truce prompted an impressive flurry of reviews and analysis, particularly on the part of the army, which hoped to learn the lessons of the conflict. Going another round with the IRA was not yet out of the question. A substantial body of histories, lectures and conference reports was produced, much of which focused on intelligence, generally identified as one of the central problems of the campaign.

The two documents reprinted (with excerpts) in this book were completed in early 1922 as part of this exercise. Both begin where the old Castle régime essentially ended: in early 1920, with the impending defeat of the RIC and DMP at the hands of the IRA. To ward off this final blow (while still attempting to avoid a major commitment of metropolitan resources) the army was temporarily given special powers of arrest while the RIC recruited British ex-soldiers to bolster its waning and faltering ranks. While these emergency repairs kept the ship afloat, new men were brought in at the top to put it back on course.

Before 1920 'British intelligence' in Ireland—insofar as it concerned Irish as opposed to foreign enemies—involved neither Englishmen nor spies.[5] While the Great War lasted British concerns were primarily with the war against Germany and the intelligence effort reflected this priority. In Britain, a vast security and surveillance machinery was built up around Scotland Yard, MI5 and MI6, the War Office and the Home Office, and the Admiralty. While all these agencies had occasional, peripheral dealings with Irish revolutionaries, they spent very little time pursuing them. The only network of agents in Ireland was primarily concerned with coast-watching and alien spies and reported to naval authorities in Queenstown (Cobh). The contrast in effort on either side of the Irish sea was nowhere clearer than in the realm of postal censorship: in Britain, MI5 had nearly 1,500 people at this task alone by the end of 1915 while Dublin Castle had to make do with fewer than ten men in Dublin and Belfast.[6]

The army's Irish Command did appoint an intelligence officer—an RIC veteran—at GHQ and in each military district (the Dublin, Midland, Northern and Southern Commands); but they depended on the police for most of their information. It was not until the army was reorganized into divisions and brigades at the very end of 1919 that unit intelligence officers gradually began to appear—albeit without extra pay or relief from other duties.

Within the Irish administration itself most of the 'political' work was carried out by ordinary policemen. County commanders routinely reported to Dublin Castle on the state of affairs under their jurisdiction, and it was their uniformed subordinates who pursued political lawbreakers and the evidence needed to convict them. Only two small groups within the Royal Irish Constabulary and the Dublin Metropolitan Police functioned as anything like a 'secret service'. Among the plainclothes detectives of 'G' Division of the DMP were perhaps a dozen men (increased to twenty by 1920) whose job it was to keep an eye on dissidents and rebels. They shadowed their targets, watched meetings, and spent a lot of their time at railway stations to see who got on or off trains. Far from being an invisible hand, such work made them well known to their targets. A few were in touch with informers but 'the G' had no spies or undercover agents.[7]

Similar surveillance work was carried out in the provinces by the Crimes Special Branch of the RIC. Despite the name this was not an Irish Scotland Yard. It was, rather, a part-time duty carried out by a sergeant at each county headquarters and by a constable at most district headquarters. These men tried to gauge the strength of political organizations (very broadly defined), recorded potentially seditious speeches and followed suspects. Half a dozen others watched the boats in Glasgow, Holyhead and Liverpool. Records were kept locally and in an office in Dublin manned by a few clerks, a district inspector and a chief inspector who nominally ran the whole operation. In practice (especially in the frantic years after 1916), the branch was often little more than the sum of its files as much of the actual work was done by whoever was available in the local barracks at the time.

These men were not specially trained nor, after 1916, did they receive special pay. They were often quite effective in collecting information but, under twentieth-century administrations (Conservative, Liberal and coalition), they made little attempt to actually infiltrate target organizations like Sinn Féin, the Irish Volunteers and the IRB, as had been done in the past. Both Conservative and Liberal policy after 1902 had dictated a less aggressive approach to political policing, and their Irish budgets made 'secret service' funds a low priority along with police pay and recruitment.[8] This, and the prospect after 1912 of a new Home Rule government in Dublin, lowered morale and discouraged initiative. Conservative and unionist commentators blamed the 1916 rising and the subsequent rise of Sinn Féin on this (as they saw it) misguided mix of liberality and frugality, and later intelligence officers echoed the charge in their own analysis of the revolution. The Liberals—and Chief Secretary Augustine Birrell in particular—'lost' Ireland.[9]

Lloyd George's coalition government and a succession of new Irish administrators changed almost nothing, despite the Easter Rising. The police were no better treated, and acted no differently. 'G' Division suffered in the cutbacks and fell below its normal strength along with everyone else. 'Secret service' funding did rise somewhat in 1917–18, but fell again after the war ended. The revitalized IRB and the militant tendency of the Volunteers—with Collins a key figure in both—were not facing a secret police or special intelligence agency. On the contrary: their targets were demoralized, underpaid, underfunded, under-manned, almost entirely uniformed and non-partisan in their duties and outlook.

It was not until late 1919 that any official undercover campaign was essayed in Dublin, in concert with one last attempt to rally the G with reinforcements from Belfast. This, apparently a joint effort between the Castle and Basil Thomson's Directorate of Intelligence in London, did make progress—incidentally revealing IRA vulnerabilities—but was quickly staunched by a new round of well-informed assassinations.

Collins would soon face further waves of British agents, however, as
well as military and police intelligence officers for the first time. This
gradually evolving new intelligence régime is the subject of the documents presented here.

The first of these is volume two of the Irish Command staff history,
A Record of the Rebellion in Ireland in 1920-21, dealing solely with intelligence (volume one concerned 'operations'). The author or authors
are unknown but presumably worked in the 'I' branch of GHQ in
Dublin. What he or they wrote is a detailed analytical history of the
intelligence effort in Ireland, including that of its two police forces, but
from a military point of view. It is the single most important—and by
common consent the most trustworthy—source we have, and the basis
for much of what historians have had to say on the subject.

Its conclusions are a litany of unsolved problems and opportunities
missed. Three main causes of failure are identified: a vacillating and
negligent government, a hostile population and a jury-rigged intelligence system lacking unity, direction or leadership. Not surprisingly,
none of this could be blamed on the army, which had to overcome years
of crisis mismanagement in a matter of months while still subject to
adverse political policies. Much of the Record's criticism was directed
at the police intelligence service, the subject of the second document
presented here.

'*A Report* on the Intelligence Branch of the Chief of Police, Dublin
Castle from May 1920 to July 1921' is the more personal (and much
less reliable) of the narratives, being written by the outstanding
character of the Irish 'intelligence community', Ormonde de l'Epée
Winter (1875–1962).[10] 'O', as he not very mysteriously code-named
himself, had joined the Royal Artillery from Sandhurst in 1894. His
career over the next two decades followed a happy, lazy trajectory
unchallenged by hard work or active service. The only action he saw
before 1914 was in England where he killed a man but was acquitted of
manslaughter. He did spend two years in Ireland (1903–5) but most of
his service was in India. Here he could devote his considerable ingenu-
ity to his enthusiasms: food, horses, veterinary surgery (self-taught!)

and pig-sticking.[11] Winter's active service finally began in Gallipoli in command of a battery, and ended in France, commanding in turn an artillery brigade, the artillery of the 11th Division, and then the division itself. He was decorated and promoted several times. By April 1920 he was a full colonel with a good war behind him.

Here the story of 'O' takes a strange turn as, out of the blue, he was appointed Ireland's first (and last) chief of intelligence and deputy chief of police. It may seem surprising that Winter, who had no experience of intelligence or police work, was chosen for such an important post at such a critical time. Nevertheless, it made sense to his friend and fellow artilleryman, General Hugh Tudor, who had been chosen to head the force, despite his own ignorance of policing or Ireland, by *his* good friend Winston Churchill.[12]

Winter generally impressed men as a dapper, if somewhat stagy, raconteur: eccentric and adventurous. Mark Sturgis, the administration's new assistant under-secretary, reported that '"O" is a marvel— he looks like a wicked little white snake and can do everything!'[13] By the time 'O' wrote his apologia, however, his aura of mystery and glamour had faded. A brief profile in *Blackwood's Magazine* in 1922 compared his appearance to that of 'the typical colonel of light comedy . . . perhaps not the best man for his present job, but hard-working, earnest, and just.'[14] Both his personality and his methods caused friction and he, like his mentor Tudor, was felt by many to be out of his depth.[15]

Winter's report was written—apparently rather hurriedly—shortly after the Anglo-Irish Treaty was signed, in late 1921 and early 1922. It describes and assesses his branch's organization and methods as well as those of the IRA (whose reputation he decries as inflated). It is also a defence of his record, already under the sustained attack detailed in the *Record of Rebellion* (which nevertheless makes use of his work). He too blames the growing intelligence 'gap' prior to his arrival on political short-sightedness and neglect and emphasizes the basic difficulty of operating within a hostile country. Furthermore, he points out, he had to build most of his organization from scratch and could not even get proper accommodation for his staff until October 1920. By Winter's reckoning, 'a marked improvement' could be seen by the spring of 1921, and his by now elaborate system was ultimately a success. The examples of success he provides rather undermine his case, however, as many are simply factually wrong.

'O' and the men of 'I' differed in their approaches to the Irish problem in two key ways. The first pitted unity against diversity. Winter defended the efficacy of overlapping or competing agencies because it preserved police autonomy, without which their work and morale would suffer. 'The psychology of the Police Sergeant must be taken into consideration.' The army felt keenly the lack of cooperation and coordination this entailed and argued that duplication was a waste of valuable time. Moreover, Winter and the police in general lacked any sort of strategic outlook and were far too localised in their efforts.

Winter's second error in military eyes was his obsession with his vaunted Raid Bureau and the stream of epitomes it produced summarizing captured documents. Where Winter saw an efficient circulation of information, intelligence officers saw frustrating centralization, as the full documents still had to be requested from the bureau and the whole process took far too much time and energy. With hindsight it can also be said that the epitomisers often distorted meanings and omitted important material.[16]

The military version of events is clearly the more authoritative. The tone of the Irish Command report is impersonal, calm, reflective: the product of the army's official mind. Its accuracy can generally be trusted, having apparently been carefully checked over by its authors and incorporating perspectives from beyond Dublin and headquarters. Winter's hurried and defensive account, on the other hand, seems to be based to a fair degree on memory and supposition. The army's instant historians did have the advantage of writing after him but he anticipated many of their criticisms and still fails to convince. This document might leave the impression that Winter was simply unsuited for bureaucratic warfare—except that he had managed to protect his turf over the previous year-and-a-half while building up a minor empire within Dublin Castle. Making enemies and increasing your staff and office space are signs of civil service success, not failure: if anything, Winter may have found his true calling.

These two accounts reveal an enormous amount about the inner history of British intelligence in 1920–1, its attitudes, methods and organization. And, despite their differences, both depict the Irish situation in early 1920 as one of disastrous failure on the part of a police force overmatched by a vicious and cunning foe and undermined by a weak government. It was up to the army or the Tudor-Winter team (depending on the writer), to pick up the pieces, which they more or less succeeded in doing by 1921. To read these reports properly, each of these interrelated claims needs to be assessed. How effective were the intelligence efforts of the old régime and how badly were they beaten? How effective were the new agencies and approaches? Just how proficient was IRA intelligence?

If the IRA's enemies prior to 1920 were less formidable than they are usually portrayed, they were also more successful than they are generally given credit for. To evaluate their performance properly, we need to get away from the fixation on Collins and the supposedly all-important duel in the streets of Dublin. It must be kept clearly in mind that, whatever Michael Collins was thinking, policemen were not fighting a 'war' in Ireland before 1920. They were trying to maintain law and order rather than attempting to destroy or defeat an enemy force. In fact the purpose of most of the RIC and DMP's political information-gathering was to gauge public opinion, monitor public organizations and to compile evidence against and arrest particular suspects.

The RIC's record on political intelligence was excellent throughout this period (we know very little about the DMP due to the lack of surviving records). Its well-tuned antennae picked up right away on the anti-government mood swing in the nationalist population after 1916 and accurately charted the subsequent fall of the Irish party and rise of Sinn Féin. The police were not privy to the inner workings of the new movement but they did have a good sense of the factions and strategies at play. And while the Volunteers were more opaque, and the IRB nearly invisible, local and national leaders and activists were well identified (including Collins). The attribution of most of the gun-play to a self-consciously militant minority—an inner movement—was likewise correct.[17]

The wrong-headed and futile decision to attempt conscription and arrest the republican leadership *en masse* in 1918 (for allegedly conspiring with Germany) was based on biased misinformation provided by outsiders, not by the more sensible Irish professionals. The police were, however, able to locate almost all the suspects (only just missing Collins, who was more lucky than crafty) and did bring the government back to reality by emphasising the strength of potential resistance to a military draft.

It was not all that hard to identify or arrest most rebels before mid-1920 (Collins being an exception only after May 1918). Even as late as the winter of 1920, once given permission to act, the army's novice intelligence officers found many guerrillas there for the taking, and rapidly decimated key IRA units. The challenge was to convict them and then keep them in prison. A failing judicial system and repeated, politically motivated releases of prisoners in 1916, 1917, 1919 and 1920 were the problems here, not a lack of basic information. The first army sweep, for example, ended in April 1920 with all of those captured being let out—on parole! Once Crown forces were able to circumvent the courts, run their own internment camps and ignore hunger strikes, it was a new game.

The IRA's only decisive advantage lay in the narrow realm of 'secret service': the covert competition to penetrate opposing organizations and prevent the enemy doing the same. In this game of hardcore espionage, Collins scored a hat trick. Not only did he develop well-placed agents throughout the government, he was able to turn some of the opposing players against their own side. And, by intimidating or killing detectives, intelligence officers and their agents, he protected his own intelligence department, and the movement, from being penetrated in turn. Despite repeated attempts right up to the Truce, British intelligence agencies never succeeded in infiltrating the underground.

On the other hand, what did Collins's remarkable achievements actually enable him to do? His sources rarely gave him useful operational intelligence other than warning of some raids and spies. He did not acquire any particular insight into British planning or intentions. The result was an essentially negative and partial one, largely confined to Dublin's inner circles: security from G men and spies, not from British intelligence as a whole.

So how did the new players do in the period covered by our two reports? It is difficult at this point to disentangle the record of the (increasingly anglicized) police forces from that of military intelligence, so the intelligence 'community' must be judged as a whole. And, once we move away from a focus on Dublin, its competing secret services and the byzantine corridors of Dublin Castle, the barracks-eye view looks very different.

In terms of results, the army's first offensive in the winter and spring of 1920 was a clear and clean success, largely untainted by murder and torture. It did not rely on covert action but started with police information and accumulated its own momentum as it went along. Early captures of documents and activists were quickly compounded as the intelligence officers and special branch men (especially in Munster) built up their arrest lists and turned several productive informers. Many key guerrillas were caught in this way. They were able to engineer their own escape, however, by hunger-striking Dublin Castle into submission. Defeat was turned into unqualified victory and the advancing British intelligence effort unravelled overnight as informers and suspects vanished, detectives were shot or had to be transferred, documents became obsolete and the enabling regulations were repealed.[18]

Next came the arrival of Colonel Winter and a new wave of British 'hush-hush men' in Dublin, sparking an increasingly dirty underground war which claimed victims on both sides.[19] In August the new Restoration of Order in Ireland Act funnelled 'political' cases through military courts, making convictions much easier to obtain. The stage was now set for the 'Bloody Sunday' massacre of agents and courts-martial officers (and assorted bystanders). This was a heavy blow both psychologically, in

terms of manpower, but not quite the Napoleonic masterstroke of the
Collins legend. The information it was based on was imperfect and some
of those shot had nothing to do with spying or trials.[20] Also, rather than
bringing relief, the shootings actually precipitated the worst setback yet
for the rebels at the hands of British intelligence. Military and police intelligence officers had by now identified most of their opponents. Raiding
parties were unleashed all over Ireland to round up known IRA officers
and activists and detention camps were hurriedly established to receive
the large numbers of men caught in the net. Informers sprang up once
again and arms were found in unprecedented numbers. Many guerrilla
units faced a crisis in morale and support that winter and official reports
began to predict their imminent collapse.

The reports were premature: a noteworthy example of poor intelligence producing poor policy as they strengthened Lloyd George's
resolve to seek a military victory. The IRA was shaken, but recovered
by tightening its security and its hold on host communities. Lost leaders were replaced, activists still at large went on the run and went further underground (literally where dug-outs were built), arms were
moved and better hidden, larger and more vulnerable flying columns
were broken up and a savage war was launched on suspected spies and
informers. The guerrillas also succeeded in killing quite a few intelligence officers and would-be agents. Attention on both sides now
increasingly turned to procuring the kind of field or operational intelligence that would allow successful ambushes or round-ups. Here, hon-
ours seem to have been about even, resulting in occasional *coups*, many
more failed attempts and an increasing spiral of brutal assassinations.[21]

In this contest of hide, seek and kill, British intelligence performed
more than adequately.[22] Its performance is all the more impressive
when the youth and inexperience of most battalion intelligence officers—who did most of the actual information gathering—is taken into
account (the same could be said of their opposite numbers in the IRA,
of course). These were not, for the most part, trained veterans of the
Great War or colonial service. In a time when the army was rebuild-
ing, when many soldiers were raw recruits, when reliable officers were

scarce and regimental duties were multiplied, many IOs seem to have been chosen for their expendability.[23] They were the opposite of an elite, although what was lost in status may have been made up for in imagination and daring. Such qualities were certainly needed as these men were left largely to their own devices. Local police often refused to cooperate and brigade, divisional and Irish Command headquarters staff do not seem to have been much help in the field.

Nevertheless, most IOs were able to build up an accurate picture of their enemy's organization and habits and to identify the main players in their area. Most had at least one informer within guerrilla ranks. Leading rebels and flying columns were tracked down with regularity, assassins and covert executioners found their targets, arms and documents were captured in great numbers. What they were not able to do was to crush their opponents and achieve a decisive victory. Nor, despite later protestations, was one in the offing in the summer of 1921. Violence was still on the rise, the nationalist population was not about to forsake Sinn Féin, and the guerrillas remained willing and vital in spirit and flesh. Time simply ran out. In the months leading up to the Truce, neither side was able to maintain any real advantage in either military or intelligence terms.

Thus, as we move from the memo-writers to the men in the field, the contest looks different, more balanced: a not unfamiliar picture, perhaps, of British unpreparedness, improvisation and muddling through. Why then, the near-universal impression of failure? The problem stems from three distortions in focus. The first, on the Irish side of the conflict, comes with the overwhelming attention paid to Michael Collins and his immediate circle. Collins was brilliant—although not quite the soldier and strategist of the standard portrayal—but we need to scrape away the layers of mythology and idolization that have encrusted his reputation, and we must be aware of the limits of his reach. His secret service may well have bested its vaunted rivals, but theirs was one battle, not the whole war.

Second, while historians have naturally embraced newly available documents from the Irish administration, the Irish Command and the

Cabinet and War Offices, we must be wary of the inherent tendency of such internal correspondence to magnify internal problems. All organizations and campaigns look problematic and conflict-ridden from the inside. This focus on central agencies and headquarters has also meant that, once again, historians have tended to overemphasize goings-on in Dublin rather than balance this against what was actually happening at the operational level throughout Ireland. Ironically, Ormonde Winter was criticized for doing the same thing.

Thirdly, intelligence gathering must not be confused with the decision-making it served. Sometimes, as with the 'German plot' arrests, badly delivered and inaccurate information (from sources other than Irish officials) produced counter-productive results.[24] More often, fairly reliable intelligence was trumped by prejudice and miscalculation. The influential belief—shared by many in Dublin Castle and the cabinet—that the real source of rebellion (as opposed to the armed struggle) was a tiny 'murder gang' ignored the police reports of the spread and depth of the republican movement and nationalist anger. The frequent early releases of prisoners between 1916 and 1920 ignored police recommendations to keep in jail those classified as 'dangerous'. The abandonment of the army's counter-insurgency effort in April 1920 effectively threw away a growing intelligence advantage (at least in the south).

Just as it is necessary to distinguish between places—Ireland was not Dublin writ large—so we must also, in measuring success or failure, distinguish between intelligence organizations and between successive phases of the revolution. Whether we look at the 1916–21 period as a whole, or just 1920–21, the intelligence war was a see-saw struggle with both sides landing effective blows and enjoying periods of success alternating with bouts of failure. The balance of information tilted both ways over time.

Finally, one vital dimension of 'intelligence' missing from the two documents presented here—and from most historical analysis—is that of politics. Many of the well-known events of the intelligence 'war' occurred as part of a particular political agenda rather than (or as well as) for military reasons. The assassination campaign of 1919–20 included overtly political targets and was part of an Ireland-wide strug-gle *within* the Volunteers to push the movement into open revolt. 'Bloody Sunday' was made as spectacular as possible, and intended to coincide with attacks on property in Britain, as much to demonstrate Irish resolve as to tackle the specific problem of the agents involved. In provincial Ireland, the 'war on informers' typically targeted those seen as political or socially deviant and often missed those closer to home who posed far more of a danger. Protestants, ex-soldiers and itinerants were the chief victims in this hidden war on minorities.[25]

On the British side, our documents record how intelligence efforts were continuously affected (and deflected) by shifts in policy, usually with the aim of conciliating nationalist opinion. However, by late 1920 elements in the security forces were mounting a parallel underground effort to terrorize the republican movement and its supporters into submission. To what extent this was a spontaneous development toler-ated from above, or a secret strategy directed from London, is unclear. What is clear is that 'intelligence' encompassed political murders and death squads on both sides. Covert operations took a more directly political form with Assistant Under-Secretary 'Andy' Cope's back-channel contacts with republican leaders and consequent extension to them of *de facto* immunity. Paul Bew has suggested that British intelli-gence was so ascendant by the spring of 1921 that it could manipulate these increasingly vulnerable men into an amenable negotiating posi-tion.[26] Whether or not this proposition will be upheld by further research, it is clear that the government had a far better grasp of their opponents' positions and weaknesses during the Treaty negotiations than vice-versa. In sum, intelligence cannot be abstracted from its political context and presented as a merely technical exercise in infor-mation gathering.

What happened to these reports and the men who wrote them? Following the Anglo-Irish Treaty, Ormonde Winter was appointed by the Irish Office as the director of resettlement for ex-policemen. By 1924 he had retired to private life where a variety of personal adven-tures and political forays culminated in his volunteering for anti-Soviet duty in Finland in 1940. He published several books including a lively memoir, *Winter's Tale* (1955), which includes a chapter on his Irish experiences (drawing heavily on his original report). It has become a standard source for the history of the Irish revolution. The anonymous headquarters men who wrote the Irish Command reports cannot be traced in later intelligence records. For most soldiers, it seems to have been a bitter experience to be forgotten as soon as possible.

Unfortunately for later counter-insurgency campaigners, their impressive body of written work appears to have been just as quickly forgotten after the withdrawal from southern Ireland, and their hard-won conclusions had to be painfully re-learned in Palestine and else-where.[27] It is instead historians who have benefited, as volume after volume has been de-classified in the Public Record Office in London or decanted into museum collections among the personal papers of departed generals. Rarely has the secret life of the British state been so exposed to inquiry as is now possible with these confidential histories.

Editorial note

A Record of the Rebellion in Ireland in 1920–21: For reasons of space and relevance I have omitted the introduction dealing with events prior to 1920, portions of chapter 2 dealing with censorship, publicity and the structure of the IRA, part of chapter 3 on topography and the 1921 Truce, and an appendix dealing with the Irish Republican Brotherhood. The Record was printed, but the print run is unknown.

A Report on the Intelligence Branch of the Chief of Police: The same IRB appendix that was excised in the first narrative has been removed here as well. Otherwise, only references to photographs have been left out. The original report was typewritten with corrections and critical marginalia added by an unknown hand (possibly a contributor to the first document).

A Record of the Rebellion In Ireland in 1920–21, and the Part Played by the Army in Dealing with It (Intelligence)

[Imperial War Museum, Sir Hugh Jeudwine Papers, 72/82/2]

The Development and Organisation of Intelligence in Ireland in 1920–21

General

It will be convenient, before considering the development and organisation of intelligence, both military and police, in such areas as it is
desirable to deal with in any detail, to review briefly the organisation
of Irish intelligence as a whole during the period January, 1920 to July,
1921.

As has already been seen the police service of information had practically broken down by December, 1919, owing to the murder of the
best and most active members of the R.I.C. and D.M.P.[1] About this
time the general policy was changing, and the Government were
inclined to allow the military to take a much larger share than hereto-
fore in restoring law and order in the country. It was realised that
guerilla warfare was the only military action to be expected on the part
of the I.R.A. and that a general rebellion was unlikely, and the necessity for a military intelligence organisation working on independent
lines became apparent. This realisation was helped by the appointment
of a trained General Staff officer for 'I' duties at G.H.Q., and by incidents which showed that the troops themselves were likely to become,
more and more, the objects of Sinn Féin attacks, while the effectiveness
of such an organisation was greatly helped by the indignation of the military forces towards the murder campaign instituted by Sinn Féin.

It was not, however, understood how completely the R.I.C. service
of information was paralysed until it was decided to arrest, about the
end of January, 1920, a large number of Sinn Féiners in the hope that
the deportation of a few hundreds would put a stop to the Sinn Féin
movement. It was then found that the local R.I.C. could give little reliable information about such persons beyond a statement that so and so
was 'a bad boy' or 'a bad article.' The police lists were out of date and

to them every Sinn Féin club was a battalion. The lists were eventually compiled with their assistance, but the I.R.A. status of the person whom it was proposed to arrest was in all cases supplied by military intelligence officers. Eventually about 60 persons (54 in the 6th Division and 8 in the Dublin District areas) were arrested on the 31st January.[2] No arrests were made by the military in the 5th Divisional area.[3]

These arrests were followed by a period of considerable military activity and more arrests, the total number up to the 14th April being 317. These were facilitated by a military raid (based on purely military information) on a Sinn Féin office in Dublin about the end of February and by the seizure of papers which gave the receipts of *'An T'Oglach'* the journal of the I.R.A., and which disclosed the names of many I.R.A. brigade and battalion commanders.

Many of the raids and searches carried out during this period were at first somewhat aimless. Battalion Intelligence Officers in the south were, so to speak, in the chrysalis stage. They were however young, keen and energetic, and, though new to their areas and to the people, soon began to get information. They were at first somewhat inclined to look on military intelligence as a kind of criminal investigation and regarded themselves as detectives. This was inevitable so long as they depended on the local 'Crimes Specials' man, but the above mentioned capture of papers in Dublin did much to make them *realise that Ireland was no exception to the rule that one's opponent's order of battle must be the principal objective of intelligence*. During March Battalion Intelligence Officers were first appointed in the 5th Division.

From the experience gained while these arrests were being made it became clearer than ever that military intelligence must depend on itself if results were to be obtained. Very considerable information about the organisation of the I.R.A. was collected; the framework of the Order of Battle was built up and it was realised that it was essential to keep up-to-date what was already known and also to discover a great deal more about those individuals who kept the spirit of rebellion alive. One of the principal duties of military intelligence was to collect information which could be used as legal advice. This combination of active operations against the I.R.A. and the trial by courts-martial or military courts of individual persons was one of the characteristics of work in Ireland and added considerably to the difficulties of the service of information. The work was analogous to the combination of 'Military' and 'Special' intelligence duties such as had been carried out under the Director of Military Intelligence during the war of 1914–18. In Ireland it was the line of demarcation between I(a) and I(b) duties.[4]

Early in April the intelligence staff at G.H.Q. was re-organised. An officer was appointed to deal with the records of each Divisional area and to ensure that the now greatly enlarged registry and card index at G.H.Q. contained all available information about I.R.A. personnel and organisation. This marked the beginning of the Irish Republican Army List.

On the 14th of this month the release of the men who had been arrested since January and who had gone on hunger strike was a severe blow to Intelligence in Ireland. It decreased still further the *moral* of the R.I.C. and correspondingly raised that of the I.R.A., whose organisation was expanded and improved. Informers, who had begun to come forward in the preceding months, now became afraid to do so and military intelligence grew both more necessary and harder to obtain.

In May a G.S.O.(1) was appointed to control intelligence in the Dublin district. Here a Special Branch had been formed to carry out secret service duties. Its existence had been recognised and regularised for some months before the arrival of this officer. It was proposed that it be extended to cover the whole of Ireland under one of the following alternatives. The first was that there should be agents working in groups throughout Ireland and all controlled from G.H.Q. The second was that all agents working in a Divisional Area should be controlled from Divisional Headquarters. It was decided, however, to give the scheme a trial first in the Dublin District only. Under the G.S.O.(1) above mentioned it achieved a very considerable measure of success, but the fact that a subordinate intelligence office was controlled by an officer of this grading tended to make the Intelligence Branch at G.H.Q. a small intelligence bureau for the Commander-in-Chief[5] rather than the directing and controlling force for intelligence throughout Ireland. Meanwhile the intelligence officers of the 5th and 6th Divisions remained only attached and graded.

In May the number of military detachments throughout the country was increased. This, besides making the I.R.A. hesitate to attack R.I.C. barracks as they had been doing for the past four months, facilitated military intelligence, for every detachment commander became an intelligence officer and the extent of intelligence areas was correspondingly decreased.

At the same time the Divisional Intelligence Staffs were increased by one officer and subsequently Brigade Intelligence Officers were graded. Battalion Intelligence officers were never graded nor did they receive extra duty pay. It is suggested that in such circumstances as obtained in Ireland all intelligence officers should have been graded higher and that Battalion Intelligence Officers, who were at least as important as assistant adjutants, should have received extra duty pay.

It was about this time that Divisional Commanders were given a sum of money to expend on secret service.

The office of the Chief of Police was formed in May. The Irish Government had decided not to proclaim Martial Law, at all events for the present, but to take all possible steps to restore the efficiency of the R.I.C. and a senior military officer was attached to the staff of the Chief of Police to deal with all intelligence questions and to reorganise the police intelligence system. It was felt that, since under the Act of 1920, the Police were to remain in existence, it would be natural and logical if the main Intelligence Branch were in the office of the Chief of Police. The intention and hope of the Commander-in-Chief was that the officer in charge of it would eventually build up a really effective intelligence system on which the military authorities could rely and on to which the existing military intelligence system could be grafted if necessary—as, for instance, if universal Martial Law were proclaimed in Ireland, when the officer in question could have joined the Commander-in-Chief's Staff as Director of Intelligence. Two things prevented the fulfilment of this intention, namely, the delay in creating the system and the fact that when it was created the Commander-in-Chief did not consider it satisfactory or one on which military intelligence could be grafted. The officer responsible himself writes 'The building up of an efficient Intelligence Service is not a task that can be accomplished in a day, a week or a month . . . The ramifications of the Sinn Féin organisation were multiple and to create a service to counter these requires an intimate knowledge of their constitutions, methods and resources. . . It is necessary to become saturated with the knowledge of the leading rebels' activities, personalities and histories. It follows, therefore, of necessity, that some delay occurred between the end of May, 1920, the formulation of the scheme and the bringing of that scheme into operation. This and the accommodation difficulty postponed any direct assumption of control to November of that year.'[6] This is an instance of attempting to build up, bit by bit, a machine that will fit given circumstances rather than adopting a sound machine and adjusting it so that it will suit circumstances. The result was an extraordinarily complex and involved organisation. Moreover, as the officer in question had no previous experience of intelligence duties, the organisation he controlled was not a purely Intelligence Branch; it undertook other duties; with the result that both they and intelligence suffered by not being carried out systematically and thoroughly. There was ample scope and a great opportunity for an Intelligence Branch scientifically organised and dealing only with the service of information.

The Commander-in-Chief eventually determined to appoint a purely military Director of Intelligence if it were ever decided to proclaim Martial Law throughout the whole of Ireland.

During the remainder of the summer of 1920 there were no changes of a far-reaching description. There were, however, gradual increases in the intelligence staffs at G.H.Q. and at Divisional and Brigade Headquarters. Practically every battalion in Ireland now had its intelligence officer and, in those units, whose strength permitted it, a scout officer who worked with the intelligence officer and assisted in most raids and searches.

The kidnapping of Brigadier-General Lucas[7] in June, and, during the following months, the attacks on troops and military convoys travelling by road (in May and June the railwaymen refused to handle military goods or carry troops over the railways) emphasised the intention of Sinn Féin to operate against the troops. These attacks became more serious as time went on and showed the effect of the release of the hunger strikers, who were the leaders and organisers of the I.R.A. The military forces were increased, but they were not yet strong enough to form mobile columns of any strength or to do more than raid or patrol in the vicinity of their stations throughout the country. Quantities of documents were seized which were of great assistance in building up the Order of Battle and completing information about the I.R.A., but it was during this summer that Sinn Féin did much to improve the organisation of the I.R.A. and elaborated their plan of campaign, which included the usurpation of the functions of the Civil Government. So many arrests were made about this time that Legal Branches had to be increased in order to deal with their work.

In August, the Government brought in the Restoration of Order in Ireland Act (commonly known as R.O.I.R.), of which the Regulations included all that was in the Defence of the Realm regulations and, in addition, gave power to try cases of murder by Courts-Martial and enabled competent Military Authorities to hold Military Courts instead of inquests. It removed many difficulties, but was not sufficiently drastic for the then existing situation, and in practice it was found that the legal procedure was too slow and cumbrous to be really effective against a whole population in rebellion. It added considerably to the work of intelligence officers who had to try to obtain evidence which the people of Ireland still refused to come forward and give.

However, the Crown Forces improved steadily during this period, more information was forthcoming and tactical methods were getting better. Various successful actions were fought, civilians were beginning to believe more in the power of the Government and I.R.A. *moral* was lowered for the above reasons and because it became clear that the Government intended to break the hunger strike weapon. In August, the Lord Mayor of Cork[8] had been arrested, tried and convicted. He determined to procure his release by hunger striking, but the Government refused to give way and after a period so prolonged as to throw doubts on the genuineness of his starvation he died in October and no subsequent efforts were made to intimidate the Government in this fashion.

By the end of the summer of 1920 the 'I' Staff at G.H.Q. consisted of:

 1 G.S.O.(2).

 1 G.S.O.(3).

 1 I.O. Class 'F.F.' (O.i/c Registry).

 4 IOs. Class 'G.G.' (Area officers).

 3 Clerks. (Increased to 7 in December).

Divisional and brigade staffs were increased by a Documents Officer and a Photographic Bureau was started in at least one Division.

Attempts were made to supplement intelligence in various ways and, amongst other things, some bloodhounds were brought over. They never achieved any success, probably because it was impossible to get enough experts to take charge of them, but they undoubtedly had some moral effect.

In October, 1920, so many of the I.R.A. were 'on the run' that they were grouped together to form 'flying columns.' Active service units were formed later. This was an astute move on the part of Sinn Féin. It provided organisations to which all *rapparees*[9] could go when they could not stay in their own areas with safety and in almost every area it created a small force which stirred the sluggish Sinn Féiners into some sort of activity and ensured terror among the remainder.

Apparently it was about this time that the I.R.A. began to realise that military intelligence was a danger to them and the kidnapping and murder of officers became part of their plan of campaign. In the south, several were kidnapped and never heard of again and on the 21st November a number of military officers were murdered in Dublin because they were, or were thought to be, connected with the intelligence or legal branches.[10] The Government accordingly decided to arrest and intern all officers and organisers of the I.R.A. on a warrant signed by the Lord Lieutenant or Chief Secretary.[11] This again increased the work of intelligence officers but the lists which had been compiled gave them far more to work on than had been the case during the early part of the year.

The first internment camp was Ballykinlar, Co. Down. Later, others were formed at Bere and Spike Islands and subsequently another large camp was made at the Curragh. Intelligence staffs for these camps were sanctioned under the guise of censors, and in some cases did excellent work. Much, however, depended on the support of the Commandant, and it was becoming increasingly difficult to find suitable intelligence officers.

The R.I.C., now, thanks to fresh recruits and increased equipment and transport, was beginning to assert itself and to patrol the country once more. Not only was it brought up to strength, but companies of auxiliary police were formed, consisting of ex-officers. It is not proposed to touch on the question of unofficial reprisals which occurred about this time beyond saying that, thanks to effective Sinn Féin propaganda, they were greatly exaggerated. Otherwise they did not affect intelligence one way or the other.

About the end of 1920 it was decided to give each divisional commissioner[12] an intelligence staff to link up police and military intelligence. Up to this time no police intelligence organisation had been created except at the Central Office in Dublin and few, if any, junior police officers had received any training in intelligence duties though there were a large number suitable and available in the ranks of the auxiliary companies. Senior police officers were all believers in local knowledge and were slow to accept new, and, as they considered, military ideas on the subject of intelligence, and not unnaturally, they were able to point out cases of mistaken zeal on the part of junior military intelligence officers. An exception to this attitude was found in the vicinities of Cork and Limerick where the liaison between the military and the police was very good, and in Limerick City the police intelligence left nothing to be desired. There was some delay in the creation of these 'Local Centres' because the Chief of Police asked for the services of a certain number of trained military intelligence officers, who could not be spared at once and who then had to spend a month studying the organisation of the Central Office and the compilation of epitomes. The first Local Centre was formed in Belfast in January, 1921. Most of the others were started in March and April in Cork, Limerick, Kildare, Athlone, Galway and Dundalk, but the Local Centre in Clonmel was not formed till June, 1921.

There was no doubt as to the scope of the work of these centres. The Chief of Police wished to centralise in them all intelligence gleaned from documents seized in their areas while G.H.Q. insisted on a clear differentiation between military and security intelligence. On the whole, they were a success; they gave the Central Office much knowledge of what was going on in the provinces and they did much to improve co-operation between the police and the military. They would have achieved even more had they been given clear and definite instructions as to their duties and had senior police officers had any conception as to what intelligence meant.

In January, 1921, the Dublin Special Intelligence Branch was transferred to the office of the Chief of Police and practically became a Local Centre but was controlled from the Central Office.

A secret service bureau, also under the Central Office, had been formed in London with the result that, including Sir Basil Thomson's[13] secret service, there were three organisations working in the Dublin District area.

In December, 1920, owing to continual outrages martial law was proclaimed in the counties of Cork, Tipperary, Kerry and Limerick, where the I.R.A. units had been more active than in any other area. Early in 1921 the remainder of the 6th Divisional area was put under martial law. This was of great assistance to the Intelligence Branch of the 6th Division, but from the general point of view of intelligence it was not a satisfactory arrangement. It tended to make this division an independent force and made any central control and co-ordination of intelligence more difficult than before. It also made it harder to effect co-operation between this division and neighbouring areas where R.O.I.R. were in force, and, as the police in the south were under the orders of the G.O.C. 6th Division, the position of the Chief of Police as regards this area was somewhat anomalous. The fact that the police were controlled by the military commander was, of course, desirable but inconvenient in that it did not obtain anywhere else in Ireland. The Proclamation also made it impossible for the police intelligence organisation to be regarded as the principal and dominating service of information in Ireland as the area under martial law was more likely to increase than diminish.

The first noticeable effect of the Proclamation was that it forced the I.R.A. to conceal their arms, when not in use, in dumps, a good many of which were discovered, for intelligence was good at this time in the 6th Divisional area and there were 45 agents, of whom 23 were believed to be reliable, working for the Divisional Intelligence Officer. These sources, however, were almost entirely dried up in February when the I.R.A., as a reply to martial law, to official reprisals and to the carrying of hostages on motor lorries, began a series of murders of persons who they believed might have given information. In every case but one the person murdered had given no information—in that one case the murdered man was an agent known to be untrustworthy, but the terror created was such that all who had been given information previously were silenced.

Another form which their reply took was a series of heavy attacks on bodies of troops during January, February and March. They inflicted heavy casualties but suffered still more severely themselves and this form of activity entirely ceased in April. Other activities were road cutting, which began in January, and ambushes of parties in trains of which the first took place in February.

Meanwhile, in the rest of Ireland there prevailed a state of anarchy and murder, as it proved impossible to capture all the leaders. Many were taken, but the chief leaders were still at large and with great determination managed to maintain the *moral* of the rank and file.

The organisation of intelligence at the beginning of 1921 was extremely complicated. There were:
(1) A large intelligence office controlling the R.I.C., D.M.P., Auxiliary Division and Secret Service, under the Chief of Police who

was responsible to the Irish Government. This was situated in the Castle.

(2) Martial law in the 6th Divisional area.

(3) Military intelligence in the rest of Ireland where R.O.I.R. were in force.

(4) In Dublin a special branch working under an officer on the staff of the Chief of Police, but attached, though not definitely or officially, to the military 'I' staff of the Dublin District for all practical purposes.

These organisations had grown up because, as has been explained, it had been considered advisable to build up the police intelligence and at the same time it was found necessary to maintain a military intelligence for the troops who were actively engaged in fighting guerrilla warfare.

The situation from the beginning of 1921 up to the Truce was that the bulk of the population was in a state of open rebellion or was in sympathy with such rebellion. All leaders of the I.R.A. were arrested or were 'on the run' and serving with the flying columns or the active service units which had been formed in the autumn of 1920. The Forces of the Crown, both military and police continued to increase in numbers and to improve in efficiency and many successful actions were fought. The casualties on both sides were heavier owing to the more energetic measures now possible for restoring law and order, but the I.R.A. casualties were proportionately greater.

In Dublin it was very difficult for G.H.Q., I.R.A., to maintain an effective organisation owing to the frequent raids. In the country by a system of military drives organised whenever any objective was reported and by strong mobile columns, the I.R.A. forces were continually hunted from place to place and were undoubtedly becoming tired and somewhat dispirited. These drives and mobile columns did not achieve any tangible or sensational results, beyond improving our knowledge of the country and training the troops and police to a system of tactics which were quite new to them after their experience of the war in Europe.

On the other hand, the double system of police and military intelligence continued to involve loss of efficiency, duplication of work and complications in almost every way. The disposal of captured documents illustrates such difficulties. In a letter dated the 7th March, 1921, the following occurs:

'Documents which do not actually form part of the Evidence against an Individual.

(a) All documents captured by the troops are forwarded to the Brigade Headquarters. All documents captured by the police are forwarded to the local centre at the Divisional Commissioner's office.

(b) The military intelligence service is responsible for dealing with all documents relating to the operations, armament, training and organisation (including the order of battle and the names of commanders and officers) of the I.R.A. After duplication of such documents they are passed in original to the police intelligence service as signatures, handwriting, typing of such papers may often be important links in a chain of evidence.

The military intelligence service transfer to the 'Local Centre' of police intelligence all documents referred to in (c) below.

(c) The police intelligence service is responsible for passing through to the military intelligence service all documents referred to in (b) above and for dealing with all documents relating to individuals, addresses, Sinn Féin police, Sinn Féin courts, Sinn Féin organisation in Great Britain and abroad, propaganda, etc., etc., and for working up the police cases against individuals.

(d) *In cases where documents form the evidence against an individual or individuals charged with possession of seditious documents*, the documents are forwarded by the local C.M.A. through the usual military channels to G.H.Q., except in the martial law area where they are dealt with by the Military Governor.'[14]

At the Central Police Intelligence Office in Dublin, where documents were of greater importance than in the country, a sub-office was formed with a staff of epitomisers in order to deal with captured documents. (There were also small epitomising staffs with each local centre.) This sub-office was termed the Raid Bureau. Its creation further illustrates the complication of intelligence in Ireland. For purposes of evidence all the documents found on the person or in the house of an individual were kept together, while, to enable the various branches of intelligence concerned to extract such information as was required, an epitome, often consisting of over a hundred typed pages, and containing a mixture of complete quotations and lists of letters was compiled. This meant that every branch had to read the whole of every epitome and then, where necessary, ask for a copy of the original. It is suggested that, with a properly organised 'I(x)' branch for all intelligence, this procedure could have been simplified.

During the first seven months of 1921 there were no further developments in the organisation of intelligence until in June when in anticipation of the proclamation of martial law throughout Ireland a Senior Officer was appointed to co-ordinate the two existing systems and to take charge of all intelligence.

The Development and Organisation of Intelligence in Dublin During 1920–1921.

(i) *Area and Population.*—The situation in Dublin was so unique that it is worth considering it in some detail. The area of the city is approximately 8 square miles, and, if the suburbs, including Kingstown, are included, the area of Greater Dublin is about 14 square miles. The population of the city is 230,000, and the inclusion of the suburbs adds about 170,000 to the above figure.

Throughout the period under consideration three G.H.Q.s existed in Dublin, namely—(1) The Headquarters of the Civil Government, including the office of the Chief of Police at the Castle;[15] (2) The Military G.H.Q. at Parkgate, at the north-western end of the City, and (3) G.H.Q., I.R.A., which directed the Sinn Féin plans as best it could from various houses in and about Dublin.

The City is divided, roughly speaking, into two equal parts by the river Liffey which is crossed by numerous bridges. It is a maze of narrow streets and alleys set in no order. There is little definite residential area, slums and tenement houses are found everywhere, and in the older part of the city there are many ramifications of underground cellars in which men, munitions and munition factories can be hidden. There are innumerable small shops and comparatively few large stores. It is in fact an ideal town for guerrilla operations.

The inhabitants are of all classes and the City is densely populated. The traders, although opposed to British rule and supporters of Sinn Féin, were openly friendly to the Crown Forces. Shop assistants and factory workers formed the backbone of the I.R.A.

All classes are permeated with mistrust and suspicion owing to the mixture of religions and politics. A considerable minority were professedly loyal but were so intimidated that they refused to give information even when they themselves had been the sufferers by I.R.A. action.

(ii) *The Organisation and strength of I.R.A. formations and units in and about Dublin*.—As was to be expected in the largest city in Ireland and the area in which the G.H.Q., I.R.A. was situated, the organisation of I.R.A. units was most complete and their relative strength greater than in any other area of the same size.

These formations and units were as follows:-

(a) *Dublin City and Dublin County, south of Dublin City*.

One Brigade consisting of four City Battalions and one 'South County' Battalion (6th). Also a 5th Battalion of which little is known. This unit was probably used as 'G.H.Q. Troops' for the defence of the G.H.Q. in Dublin.[16] Total units—6 Battalions consisting of 52 Companies. Strength—Approximately 201 officers, 4,160 other ranks.

(b) *Fingal, i.e., Co. Dublin north of Dublin City*.

One Brigade consisting of 3 Battalions or 15 Companies. Strength—Approximately 72 officers, 750 other ranks.

(c) *Co. Wicklow*.

One Brigade consisting of 3 Battalions or 13 Companies. Strength—Approximately 66 officers, 650 other ranks.

Total Unit Strength—Three Brigades consisting of 12 Battalions or 80 Companies.

Total Approximate Strength in Personnel.—339 officers and 5,560 other ranks.

In addition to the above the '*Fianna Eireann*' or Boy Scouts and '*Cumann na m'Ban*' or Women's Organisation formed auxiliary units for intelligence and communication. The latter also carried out medical duties for the I.R.A. such as first aid and nursing.

Organisation of G.H.Q.—The fact that the G.H.Q. of the I.R.A. existed in Dublin affected to a considerable degree the efficiency of the local formations and units. There is reason to believe and it is natural to suppose that the Dublin Brigade was much more under the influence of G.H.Q. than any other unit, and that some of the officers on the staff of G.H.Q. were also executive officers in the Dublin Brigade. Ambushes and bombing attacks on the Crown Forces were more numerous in Dublin than in other cities, and to a great extent this was due to the influence of their G.H.Q. Captured documents show that reports on such rebel action were systematically forwarded by the Dublin Brigade to G.H.Q., who criticised the conduct of the operations, and thus exercised a close personal supervision.

As far as can be ascertained the organisation of the G.H.Q. was as follows:-

Commander-in-Chief
Chief-of-Staff

| Adjutant General | | | | | | Quartermaster General |

Director
of

Operations	Communications	Training	Intelligence	Organisation	Engineering	Purchases	Munitions
			(Information)				

The Commander-in-Chief[17] was a purely nominal position held by the President of the Republic. When de Valera[18] was in America, Arthur Griffith[19] was President and it is possible that Michael Collins[20] then became Commander-in-Chief as Arthur Griffith had never identified himself with the military section of Sinn Féin. When Arthur Griffith was arrested, Michael Collins became Acting President, and therefore titular as well as actual Commander-in-Chief, and it was probably during this period that he gained the ascendancy which caused him subsequently to be looked on as Commander-in-Chief by the rank and file.

The relative positions of the President, the Commander-in-Chief and the Minister of Defence have never been defined clearly.

It has been almost impossible to obtain definite evidence of the actual organisation of sub-sections of the staff of G.H.Q., I.R.A. and the table shown above is an approximation from scraps of information obtained from time to time. Owing to incessant raids the leaders found it too dangerous to maintain properly organised offices and their staff work was in consequence somewhat primitive. For example, their Order of Battle (considerably out of date) was contained in a small pocket book carried about personally by the Chief-of-Staff, and the Provisional Government in February, 1922, was ignorant as to which units comprised the 2nd Southern Division.

(iii) *The Crown Forces*.——As regards the organisation and disposition of the Crown Forces, one infantry brigade was quartered and operated north of the Liffey and the other south of the river. Each had its own brigade and battalion intelligence officers, and the co-operation of intelligence and operations in the two areas of the city depended on the staff of Dublin District, which included an area considerably larger than Greater Dublin, and which, in July 1921, consisted of the counties Cavan, Monaghan, Louth, Meath, Dublin and Wicklow.

There was a Divisional Commissioner, R.I.C., in Dublin. His local centre was, however, in Dundalk, and dealt with intelligence questions connected with the counties of Louth, Monaghan, and Cavan only. Executive police operations in Dublin City were controlled to a very large extent by the Chief of Police, in conjunction of course with the G.O.C., Dublin District, both of whom had their offices in the Castle.

(iv) *Intelligence in Dublin*.——Up to the summer of 1919, the military relied for their intelligence almost entirely on the D.M.P. in the city, and on the R.I.C. in the country, but these sources were practically closed about the end of 1919 by the murder campaign. At the beginning of 1920 the military intelligence staff consisted of a junior officer, attached to the 'G' staff, whose scope of activities was very limited as he had no organised means of obtaining information. There were no battalion intelligence officers at this time, but some regimental officers, who interested themselves in the Sinn Féin movement during the summer of 1919, had got in touch with the I.R.A. This showed the possibilities of an organised military intelligence service for Dublin District and a specially selected officer took charge of this branch on 1st March, 1920. He got in touch with various civil sources of information and achieved a fair degree of success in spite of the fact that he was hampered by want of funds.

In April it was decided still further to expand and reorganise this intelligence branch, to form a plain clothes branch, and to collect both military and political information. In May a G.S.O.(1) was selected to take charge of it.

A school of instruction for suitable agents was formed in England. There they received practical and theoretical instruction on the duties they would have to carry out in Ireland. Agents were sent over in various capacities for which they were chosen according to their abilities and qualifications.

Dublin District was in the first instance divided into six areas in charge of a head agent who controlled his agents and obtained information by such means as he was able to devise. By the end of September, 1920, the system extended from Drogheda to Arklow and much useful information was obtained not only about this area but about Sinn Féin in England and about Irish secret societies in the U.S.A.

In 1921 nearly all the officers of the Dublin Brigade, I.R.A., were known, and a good percentage of them had been arrested, including the I.R.A. Director of Intelligence,[21] the head of their secret service and four battalion IOs. There were trained agents on most of the boats coming from Dublin and Kingstown. Eight of the principal departments of Dail Eireann and the I.R.A. had been raided successfully and three dumps had been taken. Twice was the G.H.Q. of the I.R.A. raided, on one occasion the Chief of Staff's personal office and plans being captured and only three days before the Truce the office of the I.R.A. police was taken.

Up to the end of 1920 this organisation, known as the Special Branch, Dublin District, worked directly under the military authorities and the co-operation between 'intelligence' and operations was most successful. The brigade intelligence officers were in close touch and themselves opened up some very good channels and battalion intelligence officers, who were appointed early in 1920, though their sources of information were limited, also achieved some good results.

The murders of the 21st November, 1920, temporarily paralysed the special branch. Several of its most efficient members were murdered and the majority of the others resident in the city were brought into the Castle and Central Hotel for safety. This centralisation in the most inconvenient places possible greatly decreased the opportunities for obtaining information and for re-establishing anything in the nature of secret service.

Early in 1921, the Special Branch with its records was handed over to the Chief of Police and amalgamated with Police Intelligence, which already had a service of secret agents directed from London. The Director of Police Intelligence was thus responsible for the organisation, henceforward known as the 'D' Branch, which had become partly intelligence and partly executive, and the Central Intelligence Office usurped functions which were properly those of a Local Centre, Dublin, which was never created. This transfer of what was in fact the military intelligence system was a grave mistake. For personal reasons it was wholly unpopular among the personnel of the Special Branch, and unfortunately personal considerations can rarely be left out of account in questions connected with secret service. The organisation continued to work for the army but was responsible to a new master, the Chief of Police, consequently the driving power behind the agents gradually diminished. The G.O.C., Dublin District, remained responsible for intelligence in an area where he had not a sufficient organisation and ceased to control the agents working in his command. Consequently duplicate organisations both to check the police information and to act as a liaison became necessary. The result was delay in taking action, overlapping in work and a registry created on the lines of compromise and satisfactory to neither military nor police.

The duties for which the various branches concerned were responsible were as under:-

(i) *'D' Branch, Chief of Police*.——Responsible for collating intelligence referring to Dublin District from:-

(a) Secret Agents' reports.

(b) Military intelligence reports.

(c) Informers' reports both from its own and military informers.

(d) Documents captured by members of 'D' Branch and by military and police on raids.

(e) R.I.C. and D.M.P. reports on the area.

(f) Scotland House[22] reports referring to the area.

(g) Passing information to Registry, Chief of Police, for filing.

Responsible for passing the collated information to the General Staff, Dublin District, for action.

(ii) *Gen. Staff, Intelligence, Dublin District*.——Responsible for keeping the G.O.C. informed of all organisation, future activities, methods and intentions of the I.R.A. and its members by –

(a) Organisation and efficient working of Brigade and Unit Intelligence Organisations.

(b) Distribution of intelligence from 'D' Branch to Brigades and Units affected.

(c) Collection and collation of intelligence from military sources, informers, prisoners, etc., and distributing such information to 'D' Branch, G.H.Q., and such military units as are affected.

(d) Advising the G.O.C. on and making out charges for the recommendation for internment of such prisoners as could not be tried by Court-Martial.

(e) Enquiring into characters of civilians employed by the military.

(f) Internal intelligence in units of the Dublin District.

(g) Keeping the Order of Battle and Army List of the I.R.A.

(iii) *Raid Bureau, Chief of Police*.——Responsible for -

(a) Filing all reports on raids.

(b) Receiving all documents, arms and articles seized in such raids by both military and police. Filing and safeguarding them so that at a future date they may be used as evidence against the owner if arrested.

(c) Epitomising such documents and distributing the epitomes to all concerned.

(iv) *Registry, Chief of Police*.——Registering all information and keeping the personal files and personal cards for all suspects. This registry was for the joint use of all branches of the Chief of Police, and for reference by General Staff, Intelligence, Dublin District.

The Special or 'D' Branch, was a peculiar organisation, as secret service organisations generally are. It was built up in the first instance by enthusiastic amateurs who neither knew nor cared about the distinctions between I.(a) and I.(b). It was partly pure intelligence and partly executive. It had its own 'constitution' and in the event of its official head taking action to which the original creators objected, they did not hesitate to raise their objections in unmistakable fashion. Persons accustomed to police or detective work, where objectives are usually limited and definite, might and did regard the personnel as amateurs. It is questionable, however, whether, if some obvious faults of organisation had been rectified, this branch would not have been as good and efficient as was possible in the peculiar circumstances that obtained and whether if it had been wisely handled it might not have been extended throughout Ireland with good results.

That intelligence as a whole obtained such good results in Dublin was due mainly to personal effort rather than to good organisation. The circumstances were peculiar and the fact that both the Director of Police Intelligence and the G.O.C., Dublin District, had their offices in the Castle, was likely to make the former see Dublin out of all proportion and to act in some respects as a local centre, in others as a county inspector rather than in his proper capacity.

If all intelligence and all operations in the City had been controlled from one office better results might have been achieved and a great deal of friction and irritation would certainly have been avoided.

*The Development and Organisation of Intelligence in Cork City During
1920–21.*

(i) *Area and Population.*—Cork is smaller than Dublin in area and its
population is much less, but it is of interest to compare its intelligence
system with that of Dublin. The area of the City is at the most six
square miles and its population is about 76,000. The military headquarters (6th Divisional and 17th Infantry Brigade) were in Victoria
Barracks on the top of a hill on the northern outskirts of Cork. In these
barracks were quartered also the two infantry battalions which were
the garrison of the City throughout the period under consideration.
Cork is divided by a river, the Lee, which has two branches that sepa-
rate near the west and re-unite about the east end of the town. They
enclose what is known as the Flat of the city, which is built on reclaimed
slob land. Consequently in this area there are few extensive cellars. The
residential area is for the most part on the outskirts of the city while in
the Flat are chiefly warehouses and shops.

The inhabitants are mainly of the lower orders and were on the
whole bitterly opposed to the Crown Forces, the proportion of loyal
people being small.

(ii) *The organisation and strength of the I.R.A. in Cork.*—Up to the time
when martial law was proclaimed there was a Brigade Headquarters
and two battalions of I.R.A. in the city. Each battalion was organised in
eight companies and the total strength was about 1,000. These battalions were at one time very good and their officer class was probably the
best in Ireland.

The position of brigade headquarters was changed frequently in consequence of the constant raids. Neither battalion apparently had any
definite headquarters. By December, 1920, when martial law was proclaimed, Brigade headquarters had been driven out of the city and were
established near Clogheen about two miles west of Cork, all documents, etc., being hidden in boxes which were buried in banks and
other hiding places. It was not long, however, before these headquarters were located and the Brigade Headquarters were then moved, first

to the south of the city and then to mountains near Macroom. Meanwhile the headquarters of the two city battalions had been broken up and no effort was made to re-establish them. When the brigade headquarters moved to Macroom a commandant was placed in charge of the two battalions in Cork City.

In addition to the battalions there was, whatever it may have been called by the I.R.A., what was neither more or less than a murder gang organised apparently in three sections. Two of these were gradually broken up and dispersed as a result of the work of military intelligence and all the members of the third were killed in an encounter with the police on the 22nd March, 1921.[23]

(iii) *The Crown Forces.*——The two battalions, forming the Cork Garrison were quartered, as has already been mentioned, in Victoria Barracks while the police headquarters were at Union Quay on the south branch of the River Lee near the east end of the Flat.

(iv) *Intelligence in Cork.*——From the beginning of 1920 there was a Brigade Intelligence Officer, the brigade area including the south and west of the county as well as Cork City. Each battalion had an Intelligence Officer, one battalion being responsible for the north and one for the south of the city. During 1920, intelligence for Cork City remained in the hand of the Brigade Intelligence Officer, much to the detriment of his work in the brigade area. It also resulted in much duplication of work and overlapping, and early in 1921 it was decided to form an intelligence office for Cork City. To this end, the two Battalion Intelligence Officers pooled their work, amalgamated their records and worked in the same office under the orders of one Battalion Commander. This arrangement proved a success in that it obviated all duplication and ensured that intelligence about the city was treated as a whole. Cork City intelligence was still further improved when a captain was appointed to take charge of the office, which became an additional and semi-independent branch of brigade intelligence. Conferences held with the police as often as was necessary, produced excellent liaison and there was no overlapping or duplication either of intelligence or operations.

The two Cork battalions were resolutely tackled at the end of 1920 and constant successes were gained against them. Ernest O'Malley,[24] an organiser from G.H.Q., I.R.A., reported in April 1921, that 'seemingly Cork intelligence owing to enemy action is badly hit for staff officers.' By July, 1921, these two battalions of the I.R.A. had ceased to function.[25]

In April, 1921, the Cork Local Centre was formed and became the Intelligence Staff for the Divisional Commissioner of Counties Cork and Kerry. This did not alter existing arrangements, and the fact that the officer in charge of the Local Centre had himself been on the staff of Cork City Intelligence ensured complete understanding and sympathy. An officer of the 'D' Branch, Dublin Castle, was attached to the Local Centre, but he was not able to increase the flow of information. This was perhaps due to the fear that he might get instructions direct and be controlled from the Central Office in Dublin.

Secret Service in a small city like Cork presented very considerable difficulties. Everyone knew everyone else and of secret service in the strict sense there was none. There were numerous informers, however, and most of them were procured by and gave their information to military intelligence. This was not surprising, as until a military officer became intelligence officer to the Divisional Commissioner in April, 1921, there was, properly speaking, no Police Intelligence Officer. As was the case everywhere else in Ireland, R.I.C. officers could not realise that intelligence was a specialist branch and that its duties were 'whole-time' ones. They all thought that they were intelligence officers and that a lifetime spent in Ireland and in the R.I.C. more than compensated for lack of training in intelligence duties and organisation.

The Development and Organisation of Intelligence in Country Districts.

There is little to add on this subject to what has already been written. The foundation stone of this system was laid when battalion and detachment intelligence officers were appointed and, as any form of central control was difficult, results depended almost entirely on the good-will and enthusiasm of these officers and the support they received from their commanding officers. Constant activity was necessary for much information was obtained during raids. Intelligence Officers had, as a general rule, to go with raiding parties themselves. This was undesirable in principle, but usually necessary in practice. The personal factor was of the highest importance. Officers who were able to establish friendly relations with the R.I.C. got, as a rule, more than those who worked independently, for although the best men, who had worked for the Crimes Special Branch in Dublin, were rarely, if ever, available, there were still many with considerable local knowledge and great experience of the country and people. The difficulty, however, was to get them to impart their information. They had been brought up to report to individuals only and were loath to tell what came to their knowledge to any whom they did not know personally, and what they knew had often literally to be dragged from them in the course of personal cross examination. This involved a great deal of the time of Intelligence Officers. Generally speaking, the R.I.C. officers, though inclined to be sceptical of military intelligence were willing to co-operate. There were only a few exceptions to this attitude. Senior officers of the R.I.C. were the most difficult to convince that there was real and urgent necessity for intelligence. They failed to realise that their own system had broken down and many of them said openly that without local knowledge nothing could be done and that all the information supplied to the military came from the police. This was not the case. In Dublin a large proportion of the information which led to results came through the 'D' Branch which was an organisation created by the military for the military, and the remainder came from purely military sources; while in the martial law area from July, 1920, to July, 1921, 85 per cent. of the operations carried out were based on military information. It must be admitted, however, that in this area the Divisional Intelligence Officer had exceptional local knowledge. The truth was that local knowledge was, of course, an advantage, but it does not need 20 years to acquire it, and it must be fortified by sound organisation and method to produce good results.

There were Intelligence Officers to Auxiliary Companies, R.I.C., but at first they had neither local knowledge nor an organised system. In some cases, however, where the officer commanding the company was an enthusiast, they achieved excellent results, and an intelligence course held for them at Divisional Headquarters in the martial law area, after the truce, proved of considerable value and showed that much might have been done by training a considerable proportion of this exceptional force in intelligence duties.

In guerilla warfare where an army is operating against practically a whole nation, where objectives are indefinite and where the peaceful peasant may at any moment become an enemy, a system of battalion and detachment intelligence officers will probably always be necessary. It is expensive, but it is unavoidable and therefore the larger the number of officers that can be trained in these duties during peace time, the easier will it be to deal with this form of warfare. Considering how few of the officers employed on intelligence duties had had any previous experience of training and when it is remembered that the system grew up almost haphazard and depended more on enthusiasm than any instructions from above, the results obtained in Ireland were remarkable. But the system was far from perfect; it was very uneven and an intelligence conference held during the truce, and attended by practically all intelligence officers in Ireland, showed conclusively that there many directions in which it might have been developed, and how much there was to be learnt by all concerned.

The Sources and Difficulties of Intelligence in Ireland, and Some of the Methods by which the Latter were Overcome.

Bad Foundations
The first difficulty was that prior to 1920 there was no intelligence organised on modern lines with complete and up-to-date records and

capable of being developed and expanded without dislocation into an effective intelligence organisation such as had been created in London and in the various theatres of war, during 1914–18.

The Crimes Special Branch depended much more on personal and local knowledge than on organisation and methodical recording. The clerical personnel at headquarters consisted of three R.I.C. sergeants and constables, all said to be excellent clerks and very keen. But they were entirely absorbed in the duties of registration, filing and indexing and were hardly ever available for typing. The card 'index' was really a series of 'history' cards alphabetically arranged. The cards were well and carefully kept, but such 'potted' records, unless produced by persons of the utmost precision and powers of concentration, are not by themselves reliable documents. The branch was all so secret that no one was allowed to know anything about it. So much was this the case that most communications for the officer in charge were addressed to him personally and were not opened except by him. The reason, no doubt, was the loathing with which any informer has always been regarded in Ireland and the realisation of his fate were his name discovered. It should, however, have been possible to have overcome this difficulty. There were many offices in London in which secrets of the highest importance were received and where there was no leakage.

Another reason was the inherent dislike of all Irish people to give information to an office rather than to a personal acquaintance, and perhaps also to some desire on the part of some members of the R.I.C. to acquire credit. Both are natural, but, from an intelligence point of view, very vicious tendencies which ought long to have been eradicated from such a force. As it was, even to the very last, it was exceedingly difficult to obtain information from almost any R.I.C. man unless he were seen and examined personally by some officer whom he knew and trusted.

The unwise economy which reduced the personnel of the Crimes Special Branch made it almost impossible to keep adequate, up-to-date and reliable records and files. Moreover, nearly every 'Crimes Special' report was laboriously written out in longhand and copies were seldom kept. They were passed backward and forward between the central and subordinate offices, thus increasing the opportunities for discovering their contents. The result was that when those men, whose knowledge would have been invaluable during 1920 and 1921, were murdered, the intelligence system in Ireland collapsed for the time being and had to be built up afresh.

Finally, the police cyphers up to a comparatively recent date were puerile. There is no evidence that Sinn Féin had an efficient crypto-graphic branch, but on one occasion at least a key to the police cypher was found in their possession.[26] This indicates that the system for safe-guarding them was inadequate.

Till the end of 1919 there was no military intelligence organisation independent of the R.I.C. and the need for and the possibilities of such an organisation were not recognised. It was not realised that the break-down of the R.I.C. system was only a question of time or that the per-sistent seizure and theft of rifles meant that the Forces of the Crown would be faced with what was in effect, whatever it might be called, guerilla warfare. Consequently, the systems which were evolved grew up haphazard and without co-ordination. In Dublin the individual ini-tiative of a few officers created what subsequently became a recognised and efficient Secret Service. In the south military intelligence depended very largely on the goodwill and enthusiasm of units. Where a com-manding officer believed in the desirability of and necessity for military intelligence, selected a suitable intelligence officer and helped him, there military intelligence usually proved efficient and successful. Above all in this area the Divisional Intelligence Officer had an unequalled knowledge of the country and was an enthusiastic supporter of battalion and detachment intelligence.

Sources of Information

(i) *Documents*.—The relative importance of the various sources of infor-mation varied according to localities. In Dublin both the military and the police agreed that their most important sources of information were captured documents. This was natural seeing that the chief offices both in Sinn Féin and of the Irish Republican Army were in Dublin.

These documents were not only the foundations on which the I.R.A. List and Order of Battle were built, but each seizure usually led to further raids and the capture of more documents until G.H.Q., I.R.A., were almost entirely demoralised. Up to 1920 Sinn Féin had taken few precautions to safeguard or destroy their papers and the documents taken in Dublin in this period were of the highest importance in that they contained more details and completer and more accurate lists of names than was the case later. It is possible that, had the importance of documents been realised in country districts, and had those captured at this time been more carefully scrutinised and analysed, the source might have proved a fruitful one, but, unfortunately, many papers were destroyed, many more were not examined, and this side of intelligence was not developed until the I.R.A. had begun to take what steps they could to safeguard themselves. From 1920 onwards the documents captured did not give full information owing to the impossibility of any methodical system of filing by the I.R.A., and in consequence of the system of decentralisation which made every I.R.A. intelligence or any other branch office practically self-contained as regards plans, operations and intelligence. Fortunately, however, I.R.A. officers often did keep documents that they could have destroyed with advantage and without loss of efficiency, and these provided excellent evidence against persons whom it was intended to try or intern. Captured cheque books led to the confiscation of about £30,000 of Sinn Féin money lodged in various private accounts.

Periodical raids were made on mails, but as has been mentioned they only very occasionally led to the capture of documents of any value.

Anonymous letters were received in large numbers, especially after it had been advertised that would-be informers could send their letters to a London address. This led to the receipt of many bogus letters and perhaps to increased intimidation. Anonymous letters were sent to every military and police headquarters and could not be neglected as they occasionally led to results, as in the case of I.R.A. officers who themselves wrote them in order to secure their arrest and removal from danger. Most, however, were the result of fear or malice.

The weak point about such documentary information was that it arrived almost invariably too late to take action. It was better from a legal than from a General Staff point of view.

(ii) *Informers.*——In their many struggles against secret rebellion the Government in Ireland have so constantly encouraged and made use of informers that now, even when he gives information against criminals totally unconnected with politics, the 'informer' is throughout Ireland held in abhorrence. This feeling made it very difficult to obtain information during 1920–21, apart from the fact that the bulk of the people were our enemies and were therefore far more incorruptible than has been the case in former Irish movements. The offer of large rewards produced no results, partly for the above reason and partly because the people were terrorised more thoroughly than has ever been the case before, and realised that it was difficult if not impossible for us to protect them. Early in 1920 it was possible to get some information in this manner, but, as time went on and the terror grew more real and was more widely advertised, informers became fewer and fewer. Information was, however, received through this source up to July, 1921. Finally, Sinn Féin realised the danger of men who drank too much. They practically stamped out drunkenness in the I.R.A. and no man who was inclined to drink was ever trusted with important secrets.

To discover informers of any value good local knowledge was essential in order to pick out those who might be able and willing to give information. The next step was to interrogate them in circumstances which did not give rise to suspicion. It was then found as a rule that some were ready to tell what they knew, frequently without asking for payment——indeed, it was found often that small presents were more acceptable than money. Women were particularly useful, but their employment sometimes involved relations that were more than friendly. This was occasionally inconvenient. Other classes which could be tapped were, the clergy (who are generally safe in Ireland whatever their religion), bank managers, shop owners and employees, military contractors, farmers and civilians employed by the military or police.

The main difficulty in this latter was to obtain the information from these people in such a way as to rouse no suspicion. Most of them had the strongest objection to putting anything on paper, and there were some who were incapable of doing so. In any case the average letter writer was redundant and verbose in style. Letters, however, were used in some cases; they were generally anonymous and marked in some way which the intelligence officer could recognise. When the post presented serious dangers letters could be hidden in some place arranged by and known to both parties, or could be handed to a trusted N.C.O. or man in a public house; but this method was rarely followed unless the N.C.O. or man happened to be the one person whom the agent trusted.

Most informants, however, preferred to tell verbally what they knew, usually to an individual officer in whom they had confidence, and arrangements had to be made to meet somewhere, conveniently near to their homes, and generally at night. In this fashion subordinate intelligence officers had a sort of local secret service, which meant considerable personal risk as they usually had to go alone to these rendezvous. A method frequently employed was to carry out a raid on and search the house of an informer, and during the course of it an opportunity could be found to speak to him or her; or it was possible to serve billeting forms on everyone in a village, and on the form given to the agent to put a series of questions to be answered. In the towns it was occasionally possible to arrest an informant during curfew hours. This, however, could not be done too often.

Many difficulties arose from the lack of funds available for area commanders and subordinate IOs to give immediate rewards. It is questionable, however, whether such funds would have overcome these difficulties as easily as the officers in question imagined because, as the terror grew, so naturally did the price of information, and the funds at their disposal must have been very considerable.

Irish persons who were prepared to act as genuine secret service agents, i.e., as Sinn Féiners or as I.R.A. were difficult to find, while Englishmen were almost impossible to employ because of their accent. A few, however, were used with success. On the whole the I.R.A.

contre-espionage was effective because of its sheer brutality. If a man were suspected he was given false information; if this was acted on by the Crown Forces suspicion became a certainty. In country districts any stranger was looked on with suspicion and, in one instance, an unknown tramp was told that he would be shot unless he confessed, in which case he would be allowed to leave the country. In the hope of saving his life the unfortunate man invented a wholly fictitious story about how he had given information to the troops, foolishly selecting an occasion when the I.R.A. had suffered particularly heavy losses. He was thereon court-martialled and shot. The whole of this incident was recounted in a letter which was captured subsequently on the dead body of the man who had ordered the court-martial and 'execution'.[27] There were very many cases where persons were shot simply because they might have given information, but on the other hand where adequate precautions were taken numerous agents were never suspected. If it were known that the I.R.A. suspected a man he had to be arrested and imprisoned or interned. If the suspicion was known to be serious the only chance of saving the man was to send him out of the country secretly and to cover his tracks successfully.

On the borders of Ulster, where a considerable proportion of the population were Protestants, information was not reliable because almost every Protestant saw a Sinn Féiner and potential murderer in every Roman Catholic.

In the south the Protestants and those who supported the Government rarely gave much information because, except by chance, they had not got it to give. An exception to this rule was in the Bandon area where there were many Protestant farmers who gave information. Although the Intelligence Officer of this area was exceptionally experienced and although the troops were most active it proved almost impossible to protect these brave men, many of whom were murdered while almost all the remainder suffered grave material loss.[28]

(iii) *Raids and Searches.*—These were a prolific source of information, both in town and in the country. They not only enabled genuine informers to be seen in safety but gave opportunities for interrogation of families of men on the run, for the seizure of documents and for chance discoveries. Most raids were the result of information or reconnaissance and were made with a definite object. Some suspected houses, however, were raided frequently. The most important points connected with raids and searches were as follows:-

As a general principle it was desirable to make a previous reconnaissance and if a house in a town was likely to lead to important results to raid another and, as far as possible, similar house in the same street so as to ascertain the type of building. Not only was previous reconnaissance desirable but a clear and definite plan for searching and guarding during the search was essential. In important raids personal and thorough searches should be made of every inmate of a house, unless they were so numerous, as in workhouses and lunatic asylums, that it was inconvenient if not impossible. Documents and weapons were hidden in most unexpected places, and in many instances were overlooked owing to sheer bluff. It was therefore necessary that those who conducted a search should have studied beforehand all available notes on the various types of hiding places.

As has been mentioned, one of the most important results of constant raids and searches was that no methodical and systematic filing or complete records could be kept in any Sinn Féin or I.R.A. office. No I.R.A. officer could feel safe at any time and enormous numbers were compelled to go 'on the run'. This in the case of a winter campaign might have had very considerable results and, in any case, compelled the I.R.A. to work in parties of some size and thus exposed them to chance of decisive defeat and heavy casualties. Sudden hold-ups and searches in the streets prevented the habitual carrying of arms and to a certain extent prevented isolated effects by small bodies of hooligans.

This subject cannot be dismissed without some reference to plain clothes work. So long as the status of the I.R.A. as belligerents was not recognised and so long as they wore no distinguishing uniform, it was inevitable that part at least of the work of the Crown Forces had to be done in plain clothes. A daylight raid, for instance, by a party in uniform was signalled long before the party had arrived on the scene of action. On the other hand a small party on one or two Ford cars could and often did arrive unexpectedly, secured their man and left before anyone had realised what had happened. Moreover a Ford car, with hood up, containing four or five men in mufti was a difficult proposition to attack, for any would-be rescuers were as likely to shoot their friend as their enemies.

Such raids were particularly effective when the names of men employed by a firm were wanted or a foreman was to be examined. Pay rolls could be scrutinised without giving any clue as to the objective of the raiders who, as often as not, were believed to be a part of the I.R.A., which is a strong argument in their favour; but it was of no use to have some members of a party in mufti and some in uniform. These small raids proved on innumerable occasions the value of surprise and boldness, provided the party worked on a definite and well-thought-out plan.

Big buildings such as workhouses and lunatic asylums were very difficult to 'comb-out'. It was preferable to carry out a raid against them on a small scale, but in that case it was necessary for every member of the party to have local knowledge and for the party to work on a plan based on information, which could generally be obtained from some discontented member of a large staff.

(iv) *Interrogation.*—The best information, i.e., that on which the most successful operations, where the heaviest loss was inflicted on the I.R.A., were based, was that given by I.R.A. deserters and prisoners under interrogation.

Interrogation is usually confused with cross-examination which is a very different matter requiring a different kind of skill. There are a few golden rules for interrogation, viz.:-

(a) *Brutal Methods are a Mistake.*—Many innocent men were imprisoned because brutal interrogators, who believed that every Irishman was a Sinn Féiner, so treated them that, in the hope of escaping further ill-treatment, they confessed that they were soldiers of the I.R.A.

(b) *Detailed Local Knowledge is Essential*, and usually the most successful interrogator was the local intelligence officer who knew about the neighbourhood or village of the man he was examining, the names of his friends and of the local I.R.A. officers. For senior intelligence officers to conduct interrogation was, with few exceptions, generally a waste of the time of all concerned.

(c) *A man should be Interrogated alone by one Intelligence Officer.*— Where two or three were gathered together was essentially not the place for interrogation, for the average Irishman will as a rule speak only to one man who to a certain extent has won his confidence. He is terrified of the idea of being overheard by anyone else, who might conceivably denounce him as an informer.

One of the reasons why it was possible to obtain more results from interrogation was that to carry it through successfully involved a considerable amount of time which the intelligence officer often could ill afford to spare on the chance of getting results. It was only a chance because the most likely subjects were not usually those who knew most. The more important a man the more likely he was to be a member of the Irish Republican Brotherhood, which is a sworn secret society, and therefore, senior I.R.A. officers were less likely to respond to even subtle interrogation than were the ordinary rank and file, though even they have involuntarily given information of value. The most suitable type of prisoner was a man who obviously was not quite certain of himself and who was worried by the position in which he found himself. Having selected a man the next step was to try to obtain some hold over him—for instance, a man who had given a false name might easily imagine that this was likely to get him into serious trouble out of which his questioner alone could extricate him. A written statement was generally useless as most prisoners were far more concerned with proving their innocence than in giving information. The man to be interrogated must be separated. He must not be with his fellow prisoners but should be visited in his own cell—not brought into strange surroundings—and he should realise that no one but his interrogator is with him and be reassured that no one can overhear their conversation. Moreover, he should understand from the first that any information he gives is sacred. It is not wise in such cases to let a man feel from the start that he is being 'pumped'. It was found best usually to commence interrogation by a general conversation about such things as the man's food, his home, or his life and pursuits about which things there is not the usual difficulty of bringing an Irishman to the point. From this it was an easy transition to the people who lived near him, and he could be asked whether he was acquainted with some one whom the interrogator knew to be locally prominent in the I.R.A. This placed a prisoner in rather an awkward predicament, for if he denied knowledge of such a one he was an obvious liar, while he did not realise where the admission that he knew the man would lead. No prisoner should be frightened with a note book. Nor should the prisoner and interrogator become too friendly.

Finally, if failure results, the interrogator must not lose his temper and above all he must never strike a prisoner.

The above is, of course, written in connection with unimportant prisoners from whom information was desired. Where a man was of importance or where his evidence was important in order to secure a conviction, a different procedure was necessary and the legal branch had to be consulted before interrogation. The claims of the law and of intelligence were bound to conflict because from a civil and legal point of view trial and conviction were all important; while, from the point of view of military intelligence, information, which might lead to operations in the field, was the first consideration.

(v) *Observations, Personal Investigation and Contact.*—I.R.A. Intelligence depended mainly on observation and it was, therefore, desirable and in many cases proved useful to adopt the same methods. Small parties of five or six which took up their position in darkness and observed, unseen, through telescopes or binoculars during the hours of daylight might with advantage have been used far more frequently than was the case. Such small parties might indeed have involved some risks, but the risks were more apparent than real, because the tactics of the I.R.A. were to ambush parties on the move when they did not expect attack, rather than to attack a party however small which was in position. In most cases such a party of well trained men would probably not have been noticed at all provided their position was well chosen. The areas suitable for observation were the mountainous and sparsely inhabited areas usually regarded as being quiet simply because they were not occupied by the Crown Forces.

In towns observation of suspected houses was equally necessary but more difficult to carry out. A stationary observer was bound himself to be noticed before long, a group of observers was obviously impossible and to make a quick and accurate reconnaissance while passing a house involves considerable skill and much training. Such reconnaissance was, however, carried out with success, especially in Dublin, during the period under review.

Self-contained and independent parties of about twelve moving about the country either in plain clothes (when they could move during the daylight) or in uniform (when their movement was by night) and travelling either on foot or in Ford cars did obtain information of value. Had more troops been available this form of activity might have been developed with advantage both from the point of view of 'Operations' and 'Intelligence'. Here again, it may seem that an unjustifiable risk would be involved. The occupants of two Ford cars, however, arrested some 40 I.R.A. officers and killed their commandant when he tried to escape;[29] while a party of one officer and 13 other ranks fought an action lasting nearly six hours with four different rebel columns, each estimated at about fifty, and retired successfully after inflicting heavy casualties. These are instances of what was achieved by small parties.

The possibilities of personal investigation depended on various factors. If an intelligence officer were well known in his area it was very difficult. In any case, he had to have a capacity for mixing with all classes. In the curious conditions which prevailed there were many forms of sport which continued during 1920 and 1921 and it was possible to pick up information both in the hunting field and at race meetings. Farmers were often willing to make friends even with officers and voluntarily or involuntarily told them much that was of interest. Some officers successfully passed themselves off as officers of the I.R.A. and obtained information of great value. This, it need hardly be said not only demanded at times courage of rare quality but always required exceptional local knowledge.

(vi) *Secret Service*.—Secret Service was on the whole a failure in Ireland. For many reasons it was practically impossible to place a man in any inner circle. For Irishmen, the risks of discovery and of its consequent results were too great; the Sinn Féin movement was so general, the proportion of Irishmen outside it so small, and any stranger in a country district so suspected that consistent, regular and unsuspected informers, such as had been employed on other occasions, were almost unobtainable at any price. The desire to inform for the sake of informing, which is such a common characteristic among secret service agents, was conspicuous by its absence. For Englishmen the work was exceedingly difficult and dangerous. Their accent usually betrayed them. If they wanted to get into inner circles they had to become more extreme than the extremists, in which case they ran a reasonably good prospect of being shot at any moment by the Crown Forces.

The Civil Government hoped and intended at one time to flood Ireland with agents. The case of Belgium was quoted. There the Germans were faced with a network of spy systems, and information was passed to the Allied Intelligence services over the Dutch border without cessation during the years 1914–18. It was at first overlooked that the Crown Forces in Ireland, and not the Sinn Féiners, were in the position of the Germans opposed by a national movement. Soon it was realised that such a scheme was impracticable and the efforts of the police intelligence were concentrated on Dublin, where, however, the vicious plan of allowing parallel systems of secret service to work simultaneously in the same area was encouraged. In spite of this remarkable results were achieved. Probably the most successful organisation was one consisting mainly of ex-officers who worked in plain clothes—mostly in the streets. They suffered heavy casualties and it was hard to get and train recruits; for a school which was started in England was discontinued, and later recruits had to receive their training actually in the course of their 'operations', thus increasing the risks both to themselves and those who were teaching them. Many otherwise suitable recruits had to be rejected because no amount of disguise could conceal the stamp of the British officer. However, men were placed successfully in most of the steamship companies trading with Dublin, on the railways, as journalists or farmers and even in the I.R.A. They made friends with Dublin citizens of every class and both sexes, they mixed with crowds and they were arrested with officers and men of the I.R.A. Their knowledge was extensive and peculiar, but it was doubtful whether owing to the system of intelligence in Dublin, they were ever employed to the best advantage.

Another branch of the secret service, based on London, is said to have cost about £15,000 a year. The information which came through this source was always 24 to 48 hours delayed and this militated against its usefulness. Moreover, owing to the police office system it was never clear from what source their secret information came and no adequate arrangements for criticism by the expert branches were ever made. This of course is a fundamental necessity with secret service.

It is laid down that lower formations should not control secret service. This, in so far as informers were concerned, had to be done in Ireland because as a rule no informer would deal with any but a man he knew. Secret service, properly speaking, did not exist in the country. Many officers believed that, had there been sufficient money available or had a secret service system been started earlier, considerable results might have been obtained. Though it would undoubtedly have been desirable for every intelligence officer to have had more money available for immediate rewards, etc., it is open to question whether money would in itself have made secret service possible; while had agents been planted five years ago throughout the country they would, assuming the policy as actually carried out not to have been altered, in all probability have become ardent Sinn Féiners by 1920.

(vii) *Listening Sets.*——Microphones and detectaphones were used to a certain extent. Their value depended on the type of building in which they were situated and they were useless in buildings such as wooden huts where every noise was magnified. Consequently, they were not effective in internment camps, but the prisoners believed they were installed everywhere, and this belief greatly hampered the I.R.A. in their attempts to escape or to communicate with their friends outside.

(viii) *Internment Camps.*——The work of intelligence officers in internment camps was hampered by their lack of local knowledge. This prevented them from interrogating prisoners successfully. Some prisoners, however, spoke freely and gave a certain amount of unimportant information.

Internés' letters were severely censored by their own leaders, and at first contained no information of value. As time went on this censorship was relaxed and letters contained political opinions of some interest but no information. The most important sources of information were the secret posts, which as they were not interrupted were believed by the internés to be perfectly secure. These letters were particularly useful especially to the branch compiling the Order of Battle and Irish Republican Army List.

(ix) *Subordinate Intelligence officers, and Rank and File and Subordinate Intelligence Staff.*——Military intelligence officers in Ireland were young, enthusiastic and extraordinarily brave and they frequently obtained excellent results by sheer audacity. Many of them developed marked aptitude for intelligence duties and proved themselves to be possessed of tact, patience and intuition. Almost without exception they were very hard workers. They had constantly to tour their areas and went personally with most raiding and searching parties, because they alone had the knowledge which ensured that raids and searches produced the best results, and they were in almost constant personal danger, for from the autumn of 1920 onwards, any officer known to be engaged on intelligence duties ran a certain amount of risk whenever he left barracks. *They proved that in guerilla war the foundation of military intelligence is the battalion and detachment system and that the best information is that obtained by front line troops.*

They had, however, some of the defects of their virtues. Zeal sometimes outran discretion and the natural and laudable determination to know their area made it difficult for them always to keep their records complete and up-to-date. This was also due to the fact that it was impossible to provide them with any clerical staff and therefore they had to do their own filing and typing.

It was also impossible in the circumstances to give them any training in their duties. Consequently, they did not always understand that it was for them to appreciate the situation from the point of view of the I.R.A. and to piece together scraps of information with a view to forecasting their enemies' probable line of action and next move, which was of the utmost importance as, in view of their mobility, it often was necessary to try to anticipate a flying column rather than to strike at the place where it was reported. Finally, their reports were not always marked by that meticulous accuracy and strict impartiality which are essential in intelligence reports.

It was probably a mistake, in a situation where the service of information was so important for all intelligence officers to be so junior, and it would have been advantageous for Brigade Intelligence Officers to have had the status of Brigade Majors or 3rd Grade G.S.O.s. As it was it was rare to find a Brigade Intelligence Officer above the rank of subaltern.

At first, intelligence officers were changed far too frequently. This was inevitable because suitable officers were not always selected. Once, however, a suitable officer is appointed and knows his area, he should not be changed save in most exceptional circumstances and, even if his battalion is transferred to another station, it may be desirable for him to remain.

Opinions as to the value of non-commissioned officers and private soldiers for intelligence duties and the use that was made of them varied in almost every unit and depended mainly on the views of commanding officers and battalion intelligence officers. It was obviously impossible to use them as agents, but there were other ways of employing them, and on several occasions, they obtained information of the greatest value, for they tapped sources which it was not always easy for the intelligence officer to reach.

Much depended on how far they were interested in and informed about the situation by means of the various summaries and memoranda which were circulated. When the men of a unit were thus interested it became possible to make use, consciously or unconsciously, of almost everyone in that unit. Results were obtained chiefly through non-commissioned officers, regimental scouts and officers' servants, through whom every scrap of information, which reached the men of the battalion in public houses, through women, etc., was passed to the battalion intelligence officer. Trained men could be employed as order-lies to prisoners, who would often talk to them, especially if an orderly appeared discontented and insubordinate. One or two scouts could always act as extra pairs of eyes to an intelligence officer during raids and searches, for the inhabitants often betrayed themselves when they thought they were unobserved by an officer, and it was a fruitful source of information to leave a man concealed in or near a house after the raiding party had apparently moved away.

Many non-commissioned officers and men were approached with offers to purchase arms. If the man approached had had some instruction such offers could be turned to good account.

Specially selected women, as usual, proved excellent intelligence clerks but the difficulty of their accommodation limited their employment.

Many more women searchers could have been employed; as it was women were practically immune from search and were known frequently to carry arms for their I.R.A. friends. The moral effect of women searchers would in itself probably have been considerable.

Ormonde Winter

*A Report on the Intelligence Branch
of the Chief of Police, Dublin Castle
from May 1920 to July 1921*

[PRO, WO/35/214]

I

Two broad fundamental facts have to be taken into consideration in dealing with the question of the Intelligence Service in Ireland: they are that, first, Ireland is an island, and, second, that there are no physical characteristics to distinguish the loyalists from the rebels. The rebellion was self-contained, and appertained only to Ireland. The activities outside Ireland were confined to the importation of arms and munitions. Obtaining financial assistance from other countries. Propaganda. Demonstrations of an operative nature in England, with a view to intimidation and as a counter-blast to the so-called policy of reprisals.

During the progress of the late European War practically no man or woman of pure English extraction was convicted of espionage, and hostile countries had to resort to the employment of aliens as agents for Intelligence purposes. This, to a great extent, applied also where England itself was concerned.

It followed, therefore, that any alien living in or visiting a country might be looked upon as a potential spy, whilst the Aliens' Restrictions Act and the Passport system enabled the authorities to exercise a certain supervision over his movements. Moreover, the spy, having gathered his information, had to transmit it to his employers, and, with the restrictions imposed on travel, he was thrown back on the postal and telegraphic services, which, in turn, were controlled by the Censorship organisation.

In Ireland, the work of counter-espionage was heavily handicapped in the absence of any of these controls. There are no means of distinguishing the potential spy from any other Irishman. The spy is able to convey his information by word of mouth, and certainly does not have to employ the postal service. The arrest of a suspect and the discovery on him of documents relating to Intelligence is, practically, the only method by which a spy can be convicted.

As applied to Intelligence in ordinary war-time, an increase in the difficulties of counter-espionage would tend to decrease the difficulties in espionage, but, as will be developed later, one fact is clear and that is, that a war-time Intelligence system cannot be employed in dealing with the class of political crime now under consideration. The information required by the War Office Intelligence Service is, to a great extent, of a different nature to that required under the circumstances under discussion. It is, moreover, more easy to obtain, and, once obtained, the information is easier to tabulate.

The passing of troop trains, the counting of guns, the estimation of forces and questions pertaining to the resources of a country can be unobtrusively obtained by casual observation: the plans and intentions of an underground organisation, information as to acts of violence committed by individual assassins, and even the order of battle of improvised guerillas dressed in the garb of peasantry cannot be obtained by onlookers or by the ordinary commercial traveller.

On the other hand, each reinforcement to the Army or Police can be counted as it arrives on the Irish shore. Our organisation is well known, and scattered as the Crown Forces are over the map of Ireland, their movements can be observed by the rebels and their plans foretold. The only correspondence necessary between the rebel organisation and other countries is that which concerns the four classes of activities above-mentioned, and, of these, the third is the only one for which the ordinary post is employed, couriers being used for communications relative to the other three.

In Ireland, the vast number of sparsely populated mountain districts and the extensive expanses of uninhabited bogs help to secure a certain immunity for the active service units that have been operating as roving guerilla bands, whilst the numerous banks, hedges and sunken roads afford nearly every route with an ideal site for an ambush on the Crown Forces, who were compelled, by reason of the dispersion, to travel from place to place.

The large number of islands, creeks and harbours have greatly facilitated the landing of arms, and the paucity of large towns renders it difficult for any agent who is a stranger to the place to remain 'perdu'.

The Irishman is of an intensely inquisitive nature, and the advent of a strange face in any village is a matter of comment from the hour of his arrival.

A captured document shows that, at a meeting of six Brigade Commandants in Co. Cork on 6.1.21, it was decided 'to arrest all strangers appearing in Areas, and make them prove their identity. In the case of a Volunteer he will be sent back to his own Area unless he either has his transfer or a note of permission from his O.C.'

It has been said that no European can fathom the mind of an Oriental, and it might equally well be said that no Englishman can fully grasp the inner psychology of the Irish rebel character.[30]

Two things tend to make this rebellious movement remarkable: one is that it has, up to the present, produced no great man, and the other is that, for the first time in history, the Irishman has not succumbed to the temptation of gold. The former is, possibly, due to the fact that, with one or two exceptions, the heads of the rebel organisation are recruited from a low and degenerate type, unequipped with intellectual education, and the latter to the fact that a surfeit of terror has replaced an appetite for gain.

II

The parsimony of Birrell[31] had resulted in the untimely demise of the Secret Service organisation, such as existed prior to his régime, whilst the Police Commission in 1919,[32] by the abolition of the extra allowance granted to Crimes Special Sergeants, had gone far to limit their zeal.

In May, 1920, the morale of the R.I.C. was at a low ebb, whilst the D.M.P., for political purposes, had practically ceased to function. Early in the year the release of the Mountjoy hunger-strikers—and, it must be remembered, a process of arrest and release had been continuous since 1916—struck a deep note of discouragement and despondency in all concerned.

A large number of brutal assassinations, without the conviction of one single murderer, the exasperating delays of the Civil Courts in those cases where criminals were arrested, coupled with the systematised boycott of the Police and their families, had led to a large number of resignations, and the position of the Police Force had become analogous to that of a demobilised army suffering from the fortress incubus. The men were immobilised behind their then ill-fortified barracks, and served but little practical use except in providing the personnel for their passive defence.

This had a far-reaching effect on the supply of Intelligence. A large number of men with local knowledge had either left the Force or been transferred for reasons of safety, and those who remained, being unable to move about, had no means of obtaining information. Persons seen holding converse with a policeman were, at best, subjected to a severe boycott, and a state of affairs had been arrived at when even the tittle tattle, open to the ordinary village policeman in England, was no longer available to his Irish confrere.

Up to this period the Army in Ireland had not been seriously interfered with, and the majority of Intelligence was derived from Military sources. Dublin District was busy organising an Intelligence system by recruiting ex-officers, and this organisation was of great value in collecting Intelligence in Dublin, which always remained the headquarters of the rebel organisation.

In May, 1920, the Commander-in-Chief expressed the opinion that a branch of the Chief of Police should be made responsible for re-organising an Intelligence system, with a view to relieving ultimately the military organisation from any responsibility in this matter, leaving the Army free to perform its legitimate functions. Two things prevented the fulfilment of this intention: one was a large increase in the activity of the rebel organisation, and the other the fact that the Army itself became a target for attack.

In considering the situation at this early period, it became apparent that an endeavour must be made to open up the well of ordinary Police information, which had run dry owing to the circumstances mentioned above, and an attempt was made to flood the country with agents, who would supply the ordinary information usually available to the Police under normal conditions. This, of necessity, was a policy that could only be developed with time, owing to the difficulty of procuring the individuals who could carry it out, but, as the months passed by, the situation underwent a change. The Chief of Police re-organised the Police, and, with vastly improved means of transport and an adequate supply of implements of war, coupled with the recruitment of the Black and Tans and the powerful addition of the Auxiliary Force, resignations became fewer, the morale rapidly improved and, at the end of six months, the R.I.C. began once more to assert itself. Regular patrolling was carried out, the personnel was no longer confined to barracks, and the ordinary channels of general Police information were once again opened. The necessity to flood the country with minor agents gradually disappeared, and it became a matter for consideration how best to augment Police information and to co-ordinate the supply of information that was gradually becoming available.

A Central Office was formed, through which all information should pass, be tabulated and disseminated. Outside Police Centres were linked to the Central Office by the formation of Local Intelligence Centres, which were responsible for collecting and passing on information between the Army and the Police, and formed the necessary branches to the main trunk. For convenience of control, these were situated at the Headquarters of Divisional Commissioners. Police information was augmented, as far as possible, by the employment of chosen agents, and a Bureau was established in London, under special cover, to deal with all sources of information other than those obtained through the ordinary channels, to collect information and pass it to the Central Bureau.

In December 1920, the military organisation employed in Dublin District was handed over to the Police, and a Local Centre was established to deal with the Dublin District Area.

The difficulty of obtaining and training suitable personnel somewhat retarded the formation of Local Centres, and the last one to be formed was only established at Clonmel a week before the Truce. Prior to the formation of Local Centres, information was distributed to the Police by cipher code, through the Crimes Special Branch, which still remained intact, and all information obtainable was sent to G.H.Q., who passed it on through the ordinary military channels. Local Centres were empowered to employ any local agents they could collect, whilst the local Police assisted in every way in obtaining local informants. These, for reasons which will be shown later, were few, but much valuable information was obtained from these sources. An Intelligence Officer was posted to each Auxiliary Company, and these, as soon as the Local Centres were established, worked in collaboration in their respective Areas.

In the month of September, 1920, G.H.Q., assisted by Scotland Yard, formulated a scheme to obtain information by correspondence. Anyone desirous of giving information was invited to do so by sending an anonymous letter to an address in London. This resulted in a quantity of letters being received, but they were practically all written either by irresponsible jesters or active rebels, and led to no satisfactory results, being, for the majority, merely accusations against well-known loyalists. The experiment was, however, well worth the attempt, as, indeed, is any experiment when faced with so many outstanding difficulties. Many other anonymous communications were received through various sources, but the vast majority contained false information, intended only to mislead.

Towards the end of 1920 a Raid Bureau, with a staff of epitomisers, was organised, with the object of dealing with the vast amount of captured documents which resulted from numerous searches, and each Local Centre, as it was formed, was provided with a small epitomising staff. Epitomes of captured documents were then circulated to all concerned, for necessary action.

Of all sources of information, undoubtedly the most valuable was that derived from the examination of captured documents. After the first important capture which, to a great extent, was fortuitous, other searches were made from the addresses noted and names obtained, and the snowball process continued, leading to fresh searches, new arrests and the obtaining of a more intimate knowledge of the plans, resources and methods of the rebel organisation, besides providing material for valuable propaganda. From August, 1920, to July, 1921, 6,311 raids and searches were carried out in the Dublin District alone.

The word of an informer is, very frequently, unreliable, but the evidence deduced from a captured document is tangible, and can generally be regarded as conclusive. It was mainly documentary evidence that enabled the authorities to obtain and hold, in face of appeals, the vast number of internees, and led to the successful prosecution of many agitators.

Endeavours were made to inculcate into all concerned the value of forwarding to the Central Bureau all documents captured in raids. Prior to its inauguration it was found that, not only was a lot of valuable information missed, but that quantities of documents were either lost or discarded as valueless. Letters seized in one part of Ireland were often meaningless, but, when compared with documents in a similar handwriting, captured in another locality, either afforded valuable clues or led to the prosecution of the writer. An instance may be cited to emphasise this point. An unsigned letter, inciting to murder, was found in the North of Ireland; and by reason of the want of signature, was retained there as being of little value. It was accidentally discovered and brought to Headquarters, and other letters of a harmless nature, duly signed, were found in Dublin. A comparison of the letters disclosed the identity of the writer, and his conviction was obtained.

Many instances might be cited, but, for a long time, subordinates conducting raids were apt to retain important documents as personal souvenirs, and relegate documents of no local interest to the waste paper basket. As the importance of this work, however, was inculcated into those who took part in the raids, these irregularities were eliminated, and, latterly, every care was taken to ensure that every document was sent to the Central Bureau for scrutiny. Certain Companies of the Auxiliary Division, R.I.C., were particularly successful in such searches.

The collation of Intelligence led to the arrest of political criminals, and their subsequent internment or imprisonment. It therefore became the duty of the Intelligence Department to supply the details necessary to formulate a charge or to warrant the action taken. A Legal Branch, with a staff of interrogators, was formed, which put up cases for internment or prosecution. This dealt with cases in Dublin District, whilst the Officers in charge of Local Centres functioned in a similar way in respect to the country, as soon as the Local Centres were established. That this entailed a considerable amount of work is shown by the fact that, in the Dublin Area alone, from the 21st November, 1920, to the 21st February, 1921, a period of three months, 1,745 arrests were effected. From December, 1920, to June, 1921, 310 revolvers, 34 rifles, 20 shotguns, many thousands of rounds of ammunition, and a large quantity of bombs, explosives, detonators and articles of equipment were captured in this Area.

III

The Crimes Special Branch of the R.I.C. had acted as the Political Intelligence System of the Force, as far as such a system—owing to manifold discouragements—was permitted to exist. The staff in the country consisted of a specially chosen sergeant at each County Headquarters, known as the Crimes Special Sergeant, and, at most District Headquarters, of a specially selected constable. Two special men were also stationed at Glasgow, Liverpool and Holyhead. It was the duty of the subordinates in the Crimes Special Staff to prepare returns of the various political organisations in their various counties and districts, to obtain an accurate knowledge of local political suspects and the descriptions of all the more important leaders, whose movements they were required to watch, and to attend meetings and report speeches, and, in fact, they were required to furnish, at any time, information as to what was going on in political circles in their districts.

Up to 1916, they received an allowance of 1/6d, per diem, but this was withdrawn by the Viceregal Commission, and, after this, with the exception of a totally inadequate allowance for plain clothes, no extra remuneration whatever was paid to them.

In spite of this, it was always possible to get men to perform this especially dangerous and distasteful duty. They were, generally, the best men of their rank at their respective stations, and but few of them shirked their duty, even when murder was an everyday occurrence.

Sinn Féin early denounced these men as especially obnoxious, and a large number of them were murdered on account of the positions they held. Others were wounded, and the lives of many attempted.

Prior to 1916, much could be obtained from local informants, though Mr. Birrell, as Chief Secretary, discouraged this as far as possible, by his reluctance to provide even an exiguous amount of money for it.[33] He was, however, fully supplied with information as to the state of affairs which culminated in the rebellion of 1916, but he chose to disregard it.

During the last two years, as has been previously pointed out, circumstances went far to impair their usefulness, but this was, subsequently, partially rectified, as the morale of the Police Force began to improve. The old records provided by this service, however, were still available, even if somewhat out-of-date.

To be suspected of speaking to or corresponding with a Special Sergeant meant certain death, and, in spite of every care, numerous civilians paid for it with their lives. For information the Crimes Special men had to rely on their own observation, such scraps as they could pick up in round-about ways and on lucky seizures and arrests. They have, moreover, frequently supplied information to the local O.C. Troops or local Military Intelligence Officer, and for this, they think, rightly or wrongly, due credit has not always been given to them. Officers in charge of Local Centres were, therefore, urged to encourage these men by personal contact, and by making them realise they were dealing with their own organisation, good results were achieved. Several men especially distinguished themselves, and the work of one, at least, may be described as brilliant.

The secret society known as the Irish Republican Brotherhood has been an organisation concerning which it has been exceedingly difficult to obtain information, and informers, members of the I.R.B., have been almost impossible to obtain. The only member of the I.R.B. who turned informer and whose information has been of the utmost value, was obtained through the agency of a Crimes Special Sergeant.

The future prospects of these men, under the new régime, are precarious in the extreme, and it is not considered likely that very many of them can remain in Ireland with any degree of safety to themselves or their families. They have certainly merited the most generous treatment that the Government can give them.

IV

As has been previously pointed out, there is but little similitude between the class of Intelligence required in war time and the class of Intelligence required for the suppression of political crime. It is comparatively easy to obtain the former, but difficult to procure the latter. The Irishman is, by nature, suspicious and secretive, the loyalist has been rendered inarticulate by terrorism, and the would-be informer, with a recollection of Carey the approver's fate[34]—still a vivid memory—prefers, as one witness put it, to 'live until he dies'. Ernest O'Maille, Staff Captain, G.H.Q., writes in a report 'Companies in South Roscommon suffer severely from spy mania. The individual volunteers distrust their officers and one another.' I.R.A. Orders that have been captured lay down that 'Anyone, man or woman, found guilty of giving information to the enemy, or in any way helping or trying to help the enemy, will be shot. Anyone in either public or private gatherings of any kind discussing Irish Republican Army movements does so at his or her own peril.' Instances have occurred in which men have been convicted and executed for 'the intention to convey information to the enemy.' Barrère, when questioned upon the actions of the Committee of Public Safety, replied that 'We had but one sentiment, that of self-preservation—but one desire, to preserve our existence, which each of us thought to be threatened.

One had one's neighbour guillotined to prevent oneself being guillotined by one's neighbour.' It is a reflection of this spirit that led, no doubt, to the 'execution' of so many so-called spies. Numbers of ex-soldiers and others have been murdered during the rebellion, not so much because they were ever discovered in active espionage—indeed, few of those who were assassinated had ever given information—but they had met their deaths partly because there was a possibility that they might become informers and partly in order to keep alive the terrorism which it was considered desirable to impose. The outside public knew not whether or no the man who had been foully done to death was an agent or not. By the customary notice found pinned on his back, it was informed that he was, and, when cases of this kind were numerous, the layman concluded that the rebel organisation had almost miraculous faculties for tracing a betrayer. To speak to a policeman was attended with grave risks; for it to be known that information had been given meant death. Such wholesale terrorism was thus exercised that the promise of pecuniary reward brought but little or no result. £10,000 was offered to anyone who would give evidence leading to the arrest of the murderers of Mr. Bell[35], who was brutally assassinated in the streets of Dublin in front of a number of people. £2,000 was offered to anyone who would not give evidence but merely information concerning the whereabouts of the murderer Daniel Breen.[36] Several other offers of rewards were circulated, but there was not a nibble at the bait, and, in no single case, was any result achieved thereby. This system of terrorism was not merely confined to persons hostile or neutral to the I.R.A., but extended also to the treatment of their own forces. Volunteers were executed without compunction, and, in a letter from the Commandant, 3rd Tipperary Brigade to the Chief of Staff, complaining somewhat bitterly of desertions, neglect of duty and cowardice, he gives it as his opinion that such men should be dealt with by making 'the terror behind greater than the terror in front, by shooting all really bad cases.'[37]

To all intents and purposes, the Intelligence Service had been operating in a completely hostile country, without any of the advantages conferred by the proclamation of war.

The recruitment of agents was a matter of the greatest difficulty. Englishmen could be found who volunteered for the service, but Englishmen operating in Ireland were at a serious disadvantage. Irishmen could be found in England, but the majority of these had lived out of Ireland for some time, and had few facilities for gaining inside knowledge. The question of time was an important factor. To build up an Intelligence organisation for the investigation of political crime in a few months is, practically, an impossibility. The Criminal Investigation Department of India was in being seven years before it commenced to yield any appreciable results.

Apart from the difficulties experienced in obtaining suitable agents, there were difficulties in obtaining a sufficient number of personnel to staff the organisation. On the 27th May, 1920, the Intelligence Staff to the Chief of Police consisted of one officer. On the 11th July, 1921, this had been increased to, roughly, 150, exclusive of the Special Branch and outside agents, but this was only built up by degrees and with the passing of time.

Early in 1920, the unemployment question had not become acute in England. Many ex-officers of ability had succeeded in obtaining employment, whilst many were unwilling to serve in Ireland under the troublesome conditions existing. The War Office, at the time, could not spare officers, and the difficulty of obtaining persons with the necessary qualifications can be readily understood. Those that were eventually obtained brought a willingness to work, but, of necessity, a lack of experience in what was, to all, a new profession. During the times of greatest stress, the work of the organisation was seriously handicapped by lack of staff.

During the months of May to October, 1920, the work was at a serious disadvantage owing to lack of accommodation, and it was not until early in October, when the Chief of Police moved his headquarters to Dublin Castle, that it was possible to make any arrangements for expansion.

The wholesale murder of practically all the members of the Dublin Metropolitan Police Detective Force employed on political work reduced that Force, exposed as they were to duty on the streets, to a complete cessation of activities as far as this class of work was concerned. The Intelligence Service was, therefore, bereft of the aid of those who knew the leading rebels by sight, and who were in a position to give information and effect arrests, had it not been a life hazard to do so.

Leaders of Sinn Féin stalked the city with impunity, until the activities of the Special Branch and the Auxiliary Companies made it unwise for them to do so. Even then, these two forces were mainly composed of Englishmen, and all, at the outset, were beset with the difficulty of want of local knowledge, and there is no doubt that many wanted men grasped the opportunity to escape by reason of there being no servants of the Crown present who could identify them.

The postal and telegraph services were manifestly corrupt. Censorship of letters provided no pabulum for action, and warrants placed on the correspondence of individuals led to no results. In the meantime, the number of political offenders continued to increase. Writing of anarchists, Proal states 'All anarchists are vain. They attain a celebrity of which they are greedy, and which affords them a kind of pleasure which intoxicates them.' So many undistinguished men had risen, during the rebellion, to a higher state than they had ever hoped to attain, so many functionaries grew up, like mushrooms, in the space of a few hours on the political dunghill, that a wild ambition turned many heads and induced them to throw themselves into the political fray. Men had frequently been arrested, released, arrested and released again. Penal servitude failed to act as a deterrent, because everyone was certain that, sooner or later, an amnesty would occur, his release would be secured, and, as a reward, he would wear the martyr's crown.

The ineffectiveness of the postal service led to the necessity of conducting all correspondence either by courier or by aerial mail, which frequently caused delay and handicapped the transmission of Intelligence.

V

Every endeavour has been made to explore all channels for obtaining Intelligence, and, in general, Police information has been derived from the following sources:-

1. Agents obtained by local Police and through the agency of Local Centres.
2. Agents recruited in England and sent to Ireland.
3. Dublin Special Branch.
4. Persons friendly to the Police volunteering information.
5. Those persons who gave information whilst under arrest or in prison, with a view to escaping the punishment of their crimes.
6. Captured documents.
7. Information from ordinary Police sources, based on observation.
8. 'Moutons', placed either in prisons or in detention cells with rebel prisoners.
9. Listening sets.
10. Interrogation of prisoners.
11. Censorship of letters of prisoners in jail.
12. Scotland House.

In this chapter no reference is made to the large fund of information obtained through Army channels, which, it is understood, is the subject of a special memorandum emanating from the Military Authorities.

The agents obtained through the local Police were, generally, the result of local knowledge, and were people who they had been acquainted with in former days. They were not kept in permanent employ, but were rewarded on the value of the information as they gave it, and, from them, many excellent results were obtained. After the ambush at Cliffony,[38] information was obtained by the Police that the arms would be removed from Sligo by motor car on the 19th November, 1920, and, as a result, two cars were intercepted, on that date. In one car, driven by Linda Kearns[39]—who was subsequently sentenced to 10 years' penal servitude—were found 10 service rifles,

6 revolvers, 430 rounds of ammunition, and various other articles of equipment. The existence of ammunition dumps at Templemore, in December, 1920, was also disclosed through an agent, and led to the discovery of 13 shotguns, 31 revolvers, 8 rifles, 1650 rounds of ammunition and a quantity of explosives and detonators, whilst, in October of the same year, the Police were able to lay their hands on large quantities of explosives and ammunition in the house of Lewis Darcy, and, later on, information was received that he was about to leave by train for Dublin, disguised as a labourer.[40] The Police arrived at the railway station at the same time as he did. He was arrested and, whilst being transported back to Galway in a lorry, attempted to escape and, by one of the extraordinary decrees of fate, met his death on the same spot where, a few weeks previously, he had brutally murdered a Police Sergeant. Thus died one of the most astute criminals in the West of Ireland.

The successful round-up of a large body of rebels at Tourmakeady, in which two were killed and thirteen seriously wounded, was the result of an agent's information that the rebels were lying in ambush at this spot.[41]

Local Centres, on several occasions, were able to procure information from members of the I.R.A., and even to get agents in as members of that force. These, as a rule, received a weekly stipend, and, through them, fairly good recruits were obtained.

The system adopted by Local Centres was to employ the group system. One outside man—in the majority of cases a member of the Dublin District organisation, who was sent to the Local Centre especially for this work. He employed Head Agents, who, in their turn, recruited sub-agents. The head of the outside branch was the only person who corresponded with the Intelligence Officer of the Local Centre, except in those cases where, for personal reasons, the Local Centre Officer dealt with an agent himself. Sub-agents corresponded with the Head Agent, and Head Agents, in their turn, passed on the information to their Chief. Most of the reports were only reduced to writing when transmitted to the local Intelligence Officer.

Experiments were made in transmitting Intelligence by some of the less important secret inks, but these were found, on the whole, to be unsatisfactory, as far as the employment of local agents was concerned.

Agents have a strong objection to putting anything in writing, and, when they do so, they are apt to be verbose and imaginative, whilst the practise of frequently interviewing agents was hazardous in the extreme. Intelligence Officers moved about at considerable personal risk, and had to resort to various strategems to get into contact with the men they employed. Many methods were tried, and these had to be constantly changed.

Terrorism prevented many agents being obtained; one could not advertise the fact that agents were required, and were to report to any particular individual, and the difficulties and risks of getting into contact with suitable persons were serious for those concerned. In order to minimise, if not eliminate, the risks incurred by agents, a Bureau was formed in London, with an officer in charge who had considerable experience in dealing with espionage through the war.[42] In England, Irishmen are more easy to approach, and, when suitable people were found, they were provided with a secret ink which was considered, for all practical purposes, immune from discovery. To each was allotted a particular task, all available information on the subject was placed at his disposal, a suitable cover was given to him and, once he had left for Ireland, he corresponded with no Government official except the head of the London bureau, writing his information in the secret ink and sending his letters to a cover address. This went far to inspire a sense of security amongst those engaged on this difficult work. The risk they ran was the possibility of their becoming suspect and being planted with wrong information which, if acted on, might have disclosed their position. Fortunately, only one of these agents met with a violent end, and this was undoubtedly, the result of his own carelessness for, amongst his effects, which were examined after his death, some notes were found written in ordinary ink, and it is more than probable that he was betrayed by one of the attendants at the hotel at which he was staying.

It is not, however, easy to recruit people for this work and, during a period of some eight or nine months, only sixty, in all, were obtained and transported to Ireland. Of these, many proved unsatisfactory and had to be discarded. One, the notorious Mr. Digby Hardy,[43] proved himself a villain of the first water, but, in attempting to betray the organisation that had engaged him, his story was disbelieved, and he was treated with some contumely by the redoubtable Michael Collins, who denounced him, in front of a lot of journalists, as 'the spy unmasked'. He was ordered by the I.R.A. to leave Ireland forthwith, lost, at the same time, his luggage and his appointment. Incidentally, neither this man nor the man who was murdered were engaged through the instrumentality of the officer now in charge of the London Bureau. Disappointments there were many, as is inevitable, but, on the 11th July, 1921, the majority of the agents employed were reliable and satisfactory.

The successful round-up of William MacNamara, who was captured whilst cleaning arms, was due to accurate information being obtained through the agency of a Local Centre, whilst, quite recently, the capture of Michael Hehir, and an ex-R.I.C. Sergeant named Harrison, whilst attempting to buy arms from an Auxiliary Company at Corofin, was directly due to information being obtained as to their movements and intentions. A trap was laid for them, into which they walked, and they were arrested on a dark night in December whilst producing the money for their presumed bargain. Several successful raids have been carried out on the information supplied through the agency of the London Bureau, which has, likewise, supplied a large quantity of information concerning the rebels' plans and the movements of prominent suspects, together with their names and locations. Instances are not lacking in which, by timely knowledge of proposed ambushes, a saving of life has been effected. A good example of this occurred in a case in which an agent reported that District Inspector Robinson was to be ambushed on the 9th January, at Cappoquin, on the road to the house of a Mr. Wyse. He was warned by cipher wire on the 7th of the intended attack, and duly received an invitation to lunch, but, thinking discretion was the better part of valour, declined. On the 9th, the

Police captured three men with six guns, in a field at the side of the road leading to Mr. Wyse's residence. They were busily preparing the ambush into which, but for the timely warning, the District Inspector would, no doubt, have walked.

The Dublin Special Branch was recruited almost entirely from ex-officers, arrangements having been made by Dublin District with the War Office to this end. A school of instruction was started in London, and agents were gradually drafted over. They lived in various parts of Dublin, under suitable cover, were worked on the group system, and achieved admirable results. Their losses were heavy. A great deal of credit is due to this body, who carried on their work in the face of grave personal risk and danger.

A good instance of a successful exploit by a member of this branch can best be quoted in his own words:-

'I had information of meetings being held on certain days at a public house in Rathdrum, and decided that Tuesday December 14th would be a convenient day on which to effect a search. In an upper room I found Matthew Kavanagh, Brigade Commandant, with Patrick Kelly and Andrew Kavanagh—two of his assistants—seated at a table, busily engaged writing orders to eight or ten detachments in Co. Wicklow. The three men were arrested, and a search of their house carried out forthwith. On the table above mentioned, I found a litter of papers, all relating to I.R.A. affairs. Amongst them I found some orders, with the ink still wet, ready for despatch and dated a day or two forward. I formulated a plan for sending out these orders, in order to secure the arrest of a number of the County Commandants, to whom these orders were originally addressed. I secured a typewriter from Kynoch's, and re-wrote the orders, composing them on the lines of the orders we had just captured, but altering the details to fit with the capture of the Brigadier, whose arrest had already become known. My intention was to summon the O.C. Companies to a meeting at Barndarrig Cinema Hut at 11.45 on Sunday, 19th December. On December 18th, I sent round a Ford car containing four agents, none of them known in the district, with typed orders purporting to come from the I.R.A. Headquarters in Dublin, which I supported with authentic I.R.A. administrative orders, that I had also captured, to eight Officers at Barndarrig, Wicklow, Ashford, Roundwood, Larragh, Rathdrum, Glenealy and Avoca. The car returned at 8 p.m., and the occupants reported that the Sinn Féiners had accepted the orders and everything appeared satisfactory. On Sunday morning, I had arranged that the same Ford car was to drive up to the Cinema Hut and drop one of the agents at the Hut for the meeting, whilst five minutes afterwards another car was to follow with six of my branch, in order to arrest the Shinners. The Ford car, however, broke down within a mile and a half of the Hut, and we therefore continued the journey in the second car, but stopped, out of sight, half a mile from the place, while the agent walked to the Hut. Five minutes later we followed, and held up everybody in the vicinity, capturing the two Officers and the agent, who, of course, was found carrying a revolver. Putting the prisoners in a military lorry which, we had previously arranged, should put in a timely appearance, we proceeded to search a number of men coming out of the Roman Catholic Chapel. Amongst this crowd at least four other I.R.A. Officers concealed themselves, and, although everybody was searched, these men gave wrong names and we were unable to identify them. On our return to Arklow, we interrogated the prisoners we had taken, and found out we had, unwittingly, allowed the O.C. Larragh, O.C. Wicklow and O.C. Barndarrig to slip through our fingers. The agent, who was placed in the cell with the other prisoners, managed to secure from them, in conversation, some valuable information concerning a raid on the mails at Inch on December 10th, a robbery of gelignite in Arklow in the spring, and the hiding place of arms in Arklow and Rathdrum.'

The religious factor had some bearing on the question of Intelligence. In Ulster, the Protestant saw a rebel in every papist, and was generally inclined to give information concerning him without strict regard to accuracy, but, in the rest of Ireland, the Protestant, both lay-men and clergy, did little to assist the forces of the Crown.

The majority of loyalists remained inarticulate. There have been, however, a few notable exceptions, and to these persons all credit is due. Some of them, like the notorious case of Mrs. Lindsay,[44] have paid the penalty for their loyalty. Had it been possible to provide protection for more of the loyalists, it is possible that more assistance might have been obtained, but, with the limited number of Crown Forces available in Ireland, it was impossible for them both to protect themselves and to accede to the many requests for protection that were received.

The certainty of a general amnesty, the knowledge that that release must come, and the hope that this release would be soon, prevented many criminals who were imprisoned from turning King's evidence or giving information. A few, however, found prison régime insupportable, and volunteered information which, if proved reliable, led either to ame-liorative treatment or to their release. These releases were, generally, effected on medical grounds, in order to avoid suspicion. Some of them subsequently acted as agents, and one, who was permitted to escape, was unfortunate in incurring the suspicions of the I.R.A., and was mur-dered at night on a lonely golf course near London.[45] In the majority of cases, the class of informer was confined to the lower ranks of the I.R.A. Hales, however, a local Commandant in Cork,[46] was induced to impart the names of most of his officers, and in order to indemnify himself from the results of his information, accused the Crown Forces of torture in their endeavour to make him speak. Two other Commandants and mem-bers of the I.R.B. volunteered information whilst in prison. One dis-closed a plot to blow up Police Barracks by rolling in front of them barrels containing gelignite. The barrels were discovered and the gelig-nite seized. No suspicion, however, appears to have attached to him, and he is still a member of the Dail, and voting against the ratification of the Treaty. The other was tried by Court Martial by the I.R.A., not, how-ever, for imparting information but for embezzling their funds.

The value of information obtained from captured documents has already been discussed. In eight months over twelve hundred epitomes of captured documents have been issued, some consisting of over a hundred pages of typewritten foolscap. These have not only been of immense value in Ireland, but have also led to several arrests in England and Scotland. The names and addresses found in these have formed the basis of the majority of the raids in Dublin. On one occasion a complete list of the names, addresses and occupations of men belonging to the various companies of the I.R.A. in Dublin were found in Mulcahy's house,[47] and all these men were successfully rounded up after the murders on Sunday, November 21st. Some of them were subsequently identified as having participated in these assassinations, and suffered, at the hands of Ellis the hangman, the penalty that they so richly deserved.

It was the scrutiny of captured cheque books that enabled over £30,000 of money belonging to illegal organisations to be confiscated by the Crown, and the timely discovery of a tunnel at Rath Camp, through which the internees intended to escape, was due to the finding of a document.

Information from ordinary Police sources, in the early days, was meagre, but, latterly, improved. It must be remembered that to watch a house or shadow an individual has been well nigh impossible. This, at all times, can only be done by one or two persons, and, when this has been attempted, they have been compelled to abandon it by threats of violence.

Latterly, the cutting up of roads and breaking of bridges has rendered frequent patrolling difficult, and certain parts of the country became almost impracticable for vehicular traffic; this, to a great extent, impeded observation.

'Moutons', arrested with due 'pomp and circumstance' and bearing obvious signs of having 'resisted arrest' were cast into prison with suspects, and succeeded in building up good cases against a number of individuals, notably in the case of Bernard Stewart, alias Earnest O'Maille, the leader of the Macroom ambush,[48] in addition to extracting valuable information from them, the evidence being fully substantiated by an audient to the conversation.

Listening sets gave unsatisfactory results—they are difficult to install with the necessary secrecy, the acoustics of a cell are generally bad, and the microphone of English manufacture seems ill adapted to the Irish brogue.

Prisoners under interrogation, in the hands of a skilled investigator, frequently, unwittingly, gave information that was of considerable value, especially when the investigator assumed definite knowledge of things concerning which he was uncertain but required confirmation, and many prisoners, assuming that much more was known about them and their actions than was actually the case, made a full confession and volunteered additional information. Father Dominic was quickly induced to confess that he was the writer of the abominable letter for which he was sentenced.[49]

Closely allied to the question of Intelligence was the question of identifying prisoners. Rebels, when they became suspect in their own district, moved further afield, and prominent personages, when the country districts became undesirably warm, fled to Dublin. In order to cope with this difficulty, an identification company was formed in Dublin, by detailed specially selected policemen, with good local knowledge, from each county, as members of this company.[50] It was the duty of these men to patrol the streets, on the look out for suspects, and to scrutinise men who were arrested. In addition, soon after the inauguration of the Intelligence Bureau, a Photographic Section was formed. Each prisoner who was arrested was photographed, and these were duly tabulated. It enabled convicted prisoners, at the end of their term of imprisonment, to be more easily re-arrested should they recommence their activities, and acted as a deterrent in those cases where prisoners were released for want of adequate evidence. Moreover, it was found that the Crown Forces, during the search of houses in outlying districts, frequently obtained photographs of men who were wanted. It was directed that these, when found, should be sent to the Central Bureau for duplication and circulation. Large numbers of photographs were circulated to the Police and Military, and it is noteworthy that, whilst the personal appearance of Michael Collins was well known to the Chief of Police, Michael Collins showed himself to have no knowledge of the appearance of General Tudor.

That the rebel organisation contemplated the formation of a similar section is shown by a letter in which P. J. Lynch, of the 'Sunday Independent'[51] wrote to the Director of Propaganda. In a memo he suggests the appointment of Director General of Photographists, and volunteers his own services. He says it would require a man or men of considerable resourcefulness, coolness and daring. 'For instance, there might be a garden fete or race meeting which, I might believe, certain persons would attend whose photographs would be useful, or I might obtain confirmation of the arrival of certain persons from England or their departure from Ireland. All legal courts, especially courts martial, should be covered. This is a particularly dangerous proposition, especially for the photographer. He would require a special camera, and, in the alternative of admission to the court, useful work would be done in the way of getting snaps of persons coming or going into the court.' Mr. Lynch's somewhat sinister motives were curtailed by his internment, but photographs of members of the Police Force have frequently been found in the possession of members of the I.R.A.

An instance of the practical utility of this service is exemplified during the investigation of the murder of Captain Lee Wilson.[52] Shortly after the Bureau was installed, and when under two hundred photographs were in its possession, some twenty photographs were selected which answered to the descriptions of the murdered man's assailants. These were shown to some witnesses who could testify to the movements of certain suspicious persons in a mysterious motor car. Two persons were identified from the batch of photographs, one of whom was resident in a distant part of Ireland. The case was very skilfully manipulated by the County Inspector, and a substantial charge of murder was formulated against these men.

Prisoners writing to their friends from places of confinement occasionally disclosed items of information, and the Military Authorities in charge of Detention Camps obtained good results from a special censorship of internees' correspondence.

The authorities at Scotland House afforded the most valuable assistance by supplying information concerning rebel activities in America, on the Continent and in Great Britain, effecting important arrests, collaborating in procuring agents and by censoring letters between rebels in England, and abroad, were instrumental in adding considerably to the fund of Intelligence.

The Director of Naval Intelligence,[53] in the early days, materially assisted by the loan of an Office[r] from his department, whose co-operation was of much value.

VI

Endeavours have been made to point out some of the difficulties that confronted the Police Intelligence Service, working in a completely terrorised and, to a great extent, hostile country. The rebels' Intelligence Service, on the other hand, had the advantage of working amidst a population the greater portion of which was friendly, and, even where persons were not, information could often be obtained as the purchase of their immunity. Hotel waiters, tramway conductors, bus drivers, tap-room loafers and members of the Cumann-na-mBan were all willing agents.

At a meeting of the latter body, at the end of 1920, a motion was proposed by Miss S. Ryan that 'Cumann-na-mBan include detective work and the acquiring of information about the enemy amongst its activities', and the Hon. Secretary, Eileen McGrane,[54] writing to the Staff Captain, G.H.Q., states that, on July 15th, 'an order was issued to our branch that the services of reliable members were to be placed at the disposal of the I.R.A., for such work as despatch carrying, etc.'

The postal and telegraph services were corrupt, and the telephone services equally so, whilst instances of Government servants and members of the Crown Forces giving information to the enemy have, unfortunately, not been lacking.

Much has been said of the efficiency of the Sinn Féin Intelligence; it has even been eulogised in the Press, but, with the manifest advantages under which it worked, it is surprising that it has not been better, and many instances could be cited in which it has been entirely at fault. In respect, however, to the class of information derived from captured documents, the Sinn Féin organisation was at a disadvantage compared with that of the Crown Forces. At one period, it is true, the constant raiding of mails secured for them important despatches, but, when the ordinary postal service was abandoned for the transmission of documents relating to Intelligence, they were deprived of this means of obtaining information. The constant capture of complete offices belonging to leading rebels and the immunity to capture of those belonging to the Crown Forces was an advantage that cannot be minimised. Whilst a vast field was at their disposal for obtaining reports, the systematic tabulation of them must have presented serious difficulties. In no office, out of the many raided, has any card index system been found, and no methods seem to have been adopted to crystallise the Intelligence gained. No doubt, the unceremonious flitting of a Minister through a window, attired only in his night apparel, and the total abandonment of his Office to the depredations of the opposing forces is conducive neither to order nor method, and, if it is possible to extend sympathy to those who have been particularly devoid of it, then the seizure of a leader's entire Office correspondence each successive month is, possibly, a worthy subject for it.

This matter appears to have given them some anxiety, insomuch that the H.Q., I.R.A., issued a circular on the subject entitled 'Instructions in View of Raids on Offices', which, amongst other items, laid down that 'No documents which would lead directly to the capture of other offices or individuals are to be filed. Lists of important persons in our organisation and addresses obviously come under this head. Files should be reduced to a minimum, only such documents as are absolutely necessary for reference should be kept. Even in the case of those, a summary in rough code would do as well as the original documents and would, of course, be much safer.

'In the event of an Office being raided and material captured which would affect any other Office, the head of the raided Office is responsible for communicating at once full details of the capture, so as to enable the Offices affected to take counter measures. Carelessness in this matter must be regarded as a very definite neglect of duty.'

In spite of these instructions, however, they appear to have been extraordinarily negligent, and, in respect to the last paragraph, Mulcahy the Chief of Staff, and Collins the Minister of Finance, must have been fully occupied sending out the necessary communications.

Mr. E. J. Duggan's method of filing Intelligence Reports seems to have been to sandwich them amongst briefs and other legal documents, and, in a letter to Michael Collins, whilst enjoying the seclusion of Mountjoy, he plaintively writes 'They have not returned any of my papers yet, and, from the way they tackled them in my Office, they mean to go right through them, in which case they will run across a lot of Intelligence stuff, which I had hidden away in clients' bundles. Of course, this was the first case in which they cleared out an office like mine.'

Up to the date of his arrest by Auxiliary Police on the evening of November 25th, 1920, to his numerous activities which included those of Treasurer to Ard Fheis, member of the Dail, Judge Advocate General to the I.R.A., Loan Collector, Solicitor for the defence of prisoners, and, after his release, Chief Liaison Officer, Mr. Duggan added the position, certainly up to the end of 1919, of Head of the Intelligence. Mulcahy, writing to him on the 23.7.19, directs him to visit certain Brigades, and pay particular attention to the thorough organisation of his own service, to see other Directors and obtain from them particulars of any special or other reports that are required.

Mr. Duggan's activities, actuated, no doubt, by patriotism, do not appear to have been entirely untinged by the prospect of pecuniary gain, for, to a letter to Michael Collins in which he says 'Poor old Sinn Féin is nearly bankrupt through your blooming Loan', he receives the reply that, but for him (M.C.) 'it would not only be bankrupt but stony broke, but that, doubtless, this constituted sufficient excuse for Duggan's pushing in his bills to the all-embracing Dail.'

Amongst the many documents found in his Office were numerous espionage and counter-espionage Reports, including many statements in detail as to the habits and movements of Lord French, which, in view of the subsequent attempt made to assassinate the Lord Lieutenant, are illuminating.

Some months prior to the arrest of Duggan, about January, 1920, when Gerald O'Sullivan[55] succeeded Michael Collins as Adjutant General, the indefatigible Michael Collins seems to have taken over his duties in addition to his own, and he assumed the title of D.I., or Director of Information. Whereas, formerly, Michael Collins sent information to Duggan, his Office now became the recipient of it. Circulars were issued by him headed 'Intelligence Department' and signed 'Director of Information'. Once only can be found any allusion to the title 'Director of Intelligence', and that was found in a letter dated 2.2.21, addressed by Mulcahy to the 'Director of Intelligence' and relating to the capture of Intelligence Instructions issued by the 5th Division. It is replied to in a characteristic memorandum, typed on Michael Collins' typewriter and signed 'M.C.', not in his own handwriting, however, but in that of Patricia Hoey,[56] his secretary. That this, however, is probably a clerical error is shown by the fact that Mulcahy, in forwarding a copy of this memo to the editor of 'An T'Oglac' alluded to it as a memorandum from the Director of Information, and requests action to be taken as the D.I. suggests.

In Collins' offices have been found large numbers of Intelligence Reports, descriptions of individuals, details and numbers of Military and Police garrisons, lists of hotel waiters and night porters, and plans and sketches of Police Barracks, whilst the corruption of the telephone service is demonstrated by the reports of telephonic communications that have passed between British officials, codes and copies of the Police cipher wires have also frequently been discovered.

We find Erskine Childers,[57] acting Director of Propaganda, writing to Michael Collins on the treatment of spies. He finds evidently some difficulty in lulling the minds of the public into a state of apathy towards the continual murders, and appears to be in a quandary as to how to do so. 'Shall we', he naively questions, 'say (1) the execution of women spies is forbidden. Kitty Carroll was not killed by the I.R.A. Or (2) Kitty Carroll was killed, in contravention of orders, by the I.R.A., and that (3) Mrs. Lindsay is now in prison for giving information to the enemy leading to the death of three I.R.A.' This letter was 23.5.21, 79 days after Mrs. Lindsay had been brutally done to death. If Mr. Childers does not mind telling a lie, he is, at least, discriminating—he wants the best lie he can get.

Staff Captain Earnest O'Maille who, when arrested, declared his name was Bernard Stewart and, as such, was about to be tried for complicity in the Macroom murders when he, unfortunately, effected his escape from Kilmainham Gaol, appears to have collaborated with Michael Collins in this Intelligence work, for I.R.A. Intelligence Reports were frequently addressed to him by name. His salary, as Staff Captain, was £6.10/- a week, augmented by any perquisites that he could obtain from the pockets of murdered Cadets.

Under this head organisation were the numerous Intelligence Officers attached to Divisions, Brigades, Battalions and Companies, the Brigade Intelligence Officer sometimes being addressed as 'Director of Information—Brigade'.

Brigades, generally, acted on their own Intelligence, and only important matters were sent direct from Brigades to the Director of Information. Michael Collins passed information on to those concerned, and the first record we have of this is in a letter dated 26.1.21, from the Intelligence Department, G.H.Q., Dublin, to the new Adjutant General, signed by Michael Collins.

The I.R.A., Chief of Police passed what information he obtained on to the Brigade concerned, and, amongst the correspondence of the numerous Brigade Intelligence Officers who have been arrested, large quantities of Intelligence Reports have been found, showing that Railway employees, ex-constables, postal officials, hotel staffs, maid servants, and many others were all concerned in the duties of espionage. An example of how, sometimes, a disregard of the value of their own information led them into difficulties is found in a Report from the

O.C., 6th Battalion, 6th Cork Brigade,[58] to the Adjutant General, dated 30.1.21, which shows that the Flying Column of the 6th Battalion took up a position for an ambush at 7.30 a.m. on 28.1.21, on the Coachford Road. Nothing happened until 4.30 p.m., when word was received from the priest in Coachford that the Military were aware of the ambush. As the priest was 'against the cause and the ambushes', they took no notice of his warning. Very soon they found themselves almost surrounded and had to retire. In the retreat, according to their own account, three men were wounded and seven missing. The losses in material to the I.R.A. forces were roughly, three rifles, some shotguns and some bombs. The Report from the Officer in charge of the Military detachment who brought off this successful coup places the losses in personnel and material considerably higher than this.

Some idea of the method of extracting information by threats of violence is demonstrated in the case of a man named David Walsh, a detailed account of whose treatment was found in a captured document. He was arrested by the I.R.A., for being 'a suspicious person of the tramp class' and he was detained for two days, during which time no information could be obtained from him. In order to remedy this, he was removed to a lonely mountain, and was confronted with the parish priest and an empty grave, and informed that he was to be shot forthwith, unless he supplied them with full information concerning himself and his accomplices. If this was forthcoming, the Captain guaranteed him a free pass to Australia. The unfortunate man, with the prospect of imminent death staring him in the face, invented a bogus story as to his having met a military party on the way to Cork, and having given them information concerning a camp at Clonmult.[59] The way in which the I.R.A. Captain fulfilled his guarantee is told in the final paragraph of the document, which reads 'David Walsh was subsequently tried by Court Martial for espionage, found guilty and sentenced to be shot. The finding was duly confirmed and the sentence duly executed.'

VII

The building up of an efficient Intelligence Service is not a task that can be accomplished in a day, a week, or a month, as previous comparison with the Criminal Investigation Department of India demonstrates. The ramifications of the Sinn Féin organisation were multiple, and widespread, and to create a service to counter these requires an intimate knowledge of their constitutions, methods and resources, which can only be obtained by experience and a prolonged study of the pamphlets and documentary evidence available. To anybody, therefore, starting ab initio, before the mention of a name can have any real significance, it is necessary to become saturated with the knowledge of the leading rebels' activities, personalities and histories. It follows, therefore, of necessity, that some delay occurred between the end of May, 1920, the formulation of a scheme, and the bringing of that scheme into operation. This, and the accommodation difficulty mentioned in Chapter IV, postponed any direct assumption of control to November of that year, but a sufficient number of offices were not procurable until some weeks later. The recruitment of agents had been commenced in July, and these had already begun to function. The formation of a suitable staff to provide for the needs of the Central Bureau as well as those of the Local Centres presented many difficulties. As a precautionary measure against leakage, the personnel of the clerical staff were all selected from individuals of English extraction. Their antecedents had to be enquired into, and their references examined before being engaged, whilst those employed in some Branches required a necessary period of training before becoming available for duty. The decision to form Local Centres was arrived at an early date, and the first was established, with a Police Officer in control, at Belfast in January, 1921. In order to establish a strong liaison with the Military Authorities and, at the same time, to procure the service of Officers who had, already, some experience in Intelligence duties, it was decided, if possible, to appoint Military Officers with Police rank to take charge of these Centres, and an application was made to G.H.Q. in December, 1920, to obtain the services of Officers who had already served on the Intelligence Staff. Unfortunately, at this time, the military organisation was commencing to expand, and suitable Officers could ill be spared. Some delay, therefore, ensued, but, through the aid and courtesy of the Commander-in-Chief, this measure was, eventually, sanctioned, and the first officer arrived on the 9th March, 1921. These Officers, after being put through a course at the Central Bureau, were provided with the necessary staff and drafted into their respective Area. Including Dublin, nine of these Centres were established, but, as has been previously stated, the last of these was only formed a week before the beginning of the Truce which, for weal or woe, put an end to the activities of the Intelligence Department. It cannot be claimed that the establishment of Local Centres fulfilled all the desideratums required by the Military Intelligence Service as well as those required by that of the Police. Duplication was unavoidable. It is difficult for any servant to satisfy the needs of two masters, but it is urged that Local Centres formed the necessary connecting link between the two services, that they provided the Divisional Commissioners of Police with a staff for the collecting and collating of Intelligence, as well as for the distribution of the same. The mere fact of a Military Officer possessing the rank of a Police Officer and, indeed, belonging to that organisation, inspired the rank and file of the R.I.C. with a confidence which could not have been obtained by any Officer of purely military rank. The psychology of the Crimes Special Sergeant had to be taken into consideration. He was an Irishman, and, even to Police Officers of long service, his confidence was given with circumspection. He preferred to impart information to his own organisation rather than impart it to another Department which, he thought, might not allot him full credit for it. One case which tends to exemplify his view may be given:—An Information Report was sent out to the Police, and also to the Military Intelligence Service, as a result of which three Reports were received, giving long particulars of each of the persons mentioned in the Report. The first was received from the Crimes Special Branch, the second was received through military channels, signed by the O.C. Infantry Brigade of that Area, and, subsequently, the third arrived, signed by the Intelligence Officer of the Division concerned. Yet all three were couched in, word for word, identically the same terms. It may be said that this is an argument against duplication, but it is an argument in favour of the contention that the psychology of the Police Sergeant must be taken into consideration. Whilst there was a divided command, whilst there was a military force functioning as well as the Police force, duplication was a necessary evil, and even with an undivided command, and two distinct forces, any absorption of the Local Centres into the military machine would have been a step in a retrograde direction. It is better to waste a certain amount of energy and time in duplication than to incur a loss in efficiency, and this opinion has been endorsed by the large majority of Police Officers concerned. As has been seen, inevitable delays interfered with the progress and gradual development of the Intelligence organisation, but, with the establishment of Local Centres, a marked improvement resulted, and would have continued, had not the political situation brought it to an end.

One of the outstanding difficulties in the suppression of political crime in Ireland was the fact that the British nation was not at war with Ireland, whilst Ireland was at war with the British nation, and regulations for the suppression of rebellion were only introduced as the situation went from bad to worse. The Irishman, without any insult being intended, somewhat resembles a dog, and understands firm treatment, but, like the dog, he cannot understand being cajoled with a piece of sugar in one hand whilst he receives a beating from a stick in the other. The Restoration of Order in Ireland Act was only introduced in August, 1920, whilst Martial Law, Curfew Restrictions and limitations to the use of motor cars were only enforced as the situation became more critical. All these could better have been imposed when the policy of coercion was first determined upon, and would, probably, have prevented the situation developing as it did.

The introduction of a Carte d'identite or passport system for all persons travelling by train or boat would have had a salutary effect in restricting the movements of rebels and impeding their means of communication. The difficulties in adopting this procedure were, undoubtedly, great, but could have been overcome.

The institution of a postal censorship of all letters passing out of Ireland would have been of material benefit in curtailing the distribution of that insidious propaganda at which Desmond Fitzgerald[60] and Erskine Childers were adepts, and which did much to paralyse the actions of the Crown Forces by re-acting on public opinion in England. An eminent writer on political crime says—'Pamphlets and propaganda turn people's heads. There are poisons for the mind just as there are poisons for the body. Certain doctrines are irresistible poison to the soul. False maxims induce death as surely as venomous substances. The number of intellectual poisons is as great as that of physical poisons.'

From the Intelligence point of view, postal censorship would have given nugatory results. None of the rebel correspondence was conducted through the post. Communications to foreign countries were sent by couriers to cover addresses in England, from whence they were despatched. Amongst the papers found on De Valera at the time of his arrest was a scheme for the institution of a courier service between Ireland and foreign countries. The arbitrary censorship of many thousands of letters led to no results being obtained.

The use of secret inks such as nitrate of silver, acetic acid and urine was sometimes, though rarely, met with, but letters written in those were not sent through postal channels.

Intelligence alone cannot win a war. It is merely an aid to force, and it is only by action that the desired end can be attained. The need for action on the part of the rebels was fully realised by them. Kropotkine, the theorist of anarchism, writing on the subject, says—'It is by action that minorities succeed in awakening that sentiment of independence and that fever of audacity in the absence of which it is impossible that a revolution should be accomplished. By dint of incidents that force themselves upon the general attention, the new idea filters into men's minds and wins proselytes. An act may do more, in a few days, to spread a doctrine, than thousands of pamphlets. Above all, it awakes the spirit of

revolt—it breeds audacity. There have been audacious acts that have suf-
ficed to put the entire Government machine out of gear—they have
shaken the Colossus, the masses see that the monster is not so terrible
as they imagined, they foresee the victory and their audacity grows.'

The Sinn Féin organisation endeavoured, by systematised murder,
to terrorise the British Government. In this it failed. The British Government attempted to counter this action by a coercion which was not
sufficiently severe. By it they nearly succeeded. The great Clausewitz
said 'All kinds of philanthropy in war are a gross and pernicious error.'

It is a matter for some wonder that the atrocities committed by Sinn
Féin, unparalleled by any of those acts committed by the Germans in
Belgium, should have met with such scanty condemnation at the hands
of the Roman Catholic clergy. There are a few outstanding instances of
murders and ambushes meeting with censure, but, for the majority, the
hierarchy looked on with apathy, and in some cases, assisted and con-
doned. One Reverend Father, in a letter to a Brigade Commandant,
writes—'I address this note neither to Mr. O'Duffy nor to Mr. Daly,
but to the rank and file of those present at the meeting tonight, and, as
a priest, I ask them to consider carefully their intended actions and their
possible consequences. I understand, from more sources than one, that
Mr. O'Duffy is prepared to shoot those who oppose him. At the risk of
being shot, I do not hesitate to tell him that this course of action is indis-
creet, and that he will not be allowed to play fast and loose with the souls
and bodies of our young men and the homes of our people without, at
least, one voice being raised against it. It can scarcely be called courage
for young men with arms in their hands to ambush soldiers and policemen, fly when they have murdered them and leave civilians who have no
weapons except those which Nature gives them to the mercy of an
enraged soldiery. Until such time as the Officers at the head of the Volunteers display ordinary prudence, I call upon any Volunteer for whose
eternal salvation I am responsible to leave them, and to refuse to obey
orders.' Unfortunately, letters of this kind were rare, and seem to have
had but little effect on the minds of the rebels themselves, for the
Brigade Commandant, in forwarding it to the Chief of Staff, says—'This

priest was a prominent Sinn Féiner, but, since getting a threatening letter from the Black and Tans, has performed a somersault. His acts will have no effect on the Carduff Company.' Michael Collins also seems to have seen it, and adds his remarks—'I am not in agreement with a single line of it. The letter from the priest merely amounts to an argument against the Flying Columns. I think physical force is necessary.'

Repression could have broken the spirit of the revolt, but it is not a final solution to the Irish problem, which, from its childhood days, seven hundred years ago, has grown into a hoary-headed, intolerable nuisance. So long as oil will not mix with water, so long will the Roman Catholic remain irreconcilable with the Protestant of the North. So long as the Irish Republican Brotherhood exists, so long will there be a faction in Ireland who will fight for a Republic. The speeches of the pseudo statesmen of the Dail, the still more recent utterance of De Valera on Sunday, 8th January [1922], and the proclamation of Cathal Burgess,[61] bode ill for the future of Ireland, and to what extent the Treaty will bring the semblance of peace to this distracted nation of born agitators must, for the present, remain an unsolved problem of the future.

ENVOI

To my colleagues, in both Civil and Military Departments, who have done much to smooth over the many difficulties that have arisen, to Sir Basil Thomson, Colonel Carter,[62] and the Authorities of Scotland Yard, who have so generously assisted, to the Director of Naval Intelligence, who, in the early stages, lent his valuable co-operation, to Mr. Cheeseman, of the Crimes Special Branch, to those Officers of the Police Forces, without whose assistance the work would have been impossible, and to those members of the hard-worked Staff who served with loyalty, I take this opportunity of recording an expression of my humble but sincere appreciation and my profoundly grateful thanks.

'O'

Abbreviations

CMA	Competent Military Authority
CO	Colonial Office
DMP	Dublin Metropolitan Police
GHQ	General Headquarters (IRA)
GOC	General Officer Commanding
GSO	General Staff Officer
HC	House of Commons
IRA	Irish Republican Army
IRB	Irish Republican Brotherhood
O/C	Officer Commanding
PRO	Public Record Office, London
RIC	Royal Irish Constabulary
WO	War Office

Notes to Introduction

1   Lewis Namier, *The Structure of Politics at the Accession of George III*, 2nd ed. (London, 1957), p. 176.

2   With one main exception. In his first book, *The British Campaign in Ireland*, Charles Townshend generally accepted this narrative, but he has since substantially revised his original conclusions about republican success and British failure. In the light of more recently available IRA documents, which reveal an equally high level of uncertainty and error, 'the legendary omniscience of the IRA begins to seem more and more mythical': Townshend, 'The Irish Republican Army', p. 329.

3   Tim Pat Coogan, *Michael Collins*, xi–xii. See Townshend, *British Campaign in Ireland* and Eunan O'Halpin, *The Decline of the Union* (Dublin, 1987), which covers the period up to April 1920.

4   Peter Gudgin, *Military Intelligence*, p. 52.

5   For an overview of the intelligence community, such as it was, see Eunan O'Halpin, 'British Intelligence in Ireland', pp. 54–77. For the DMP especially, see David Neligan's atmospheric insider's memoir, *The Spy in the Castle*. For an excellent overview of the post-war military scene, see Keith Jeffery, 'British Military Intelligence'.

6   Ben Novick, 'Postal Censorship in Ireland', p. 351.

7   Some useful details of 'the G' can be found in the following official reports: *Report of the Committee of Inquiry Into the Dublin Metropolitan Police 1901*, HC 1902 (Cd.1088), xlii, 8–11; *Evidence Taken Before the Committee of Inquiry 1901* HC 1902 (Cd.1095), 8–10; *Report of the Committee of Inquiry into the Royal Irish Constabulary and the Dublin Metropolitan Police*, HC 1914 (Cd.7637), xliv, 30–1; *Evidence Taken Before the Committee of Inquiry*, HC 1914–16, xxxii, 297–300; *Report of the Vice-Regal Commission on the Reorganization and Pay of the Irish Police Forces* HC 1920 (Cd.603), xxii, 13.

8   See O'Halpin, *Decline of the Union*.

9   Although the downgrading of the perceived threat from republicans and secret societies had begun under a Conservative government. See W.F. Mandle, 'Sir Antony MacDonnell and Crime Branch Special'.

10 The following biographical details are drawn from: obituaries published in the *Times*, 15 and 20 Feb. 1962; *Who Was Who, 1961–1970*; Sir Ormonde Winter, *Winter's Tale*.

11 Winter, *Winter's Tale*, p. 168.

12 See Winter, p. 289; General Sir Nevil Macready, *Annals of an Active Life*, vol. 2, pp. 459, 462; Townshend, *British Campaign*, pp. 81–2.

13 Mark Sturgis diary, 1 Sept. 1920 (PRO 30/59).

14 'Periscope' (Duggan) 'The Last Days of Dublin Castle', p. 167.

15   See further entries in the Sturgis diaries on 15 Sept., 28 Oct., 19 Nov., 17 Dec.,
      1920.

16   For raids, see 25th Bde. Raid Reports and Raids General Files, Jan. 1920–July
      1921 (PRO, WO 35/70–72). For registers of prisoners and internees, see PRO,
      WO 35/143, 144; charges before field general courts-martial are recorded in
      WO 35/93B. Examples of documentary epitomes can be found in the Charles
      Howard Foulkes Papers (Liddell Hart Centre for Military Archives).

17   I am basing this assessment on a survey of all monthly reports by county inspec-
      tors and the Inspector General, RIC, from the years 1917 and 1918 (PRO, CO
      904/102–7).

18   For a local analysis of these events, see Hart, *The IRA and Its Enemies*, pp. 73–5.

19   The phrase is Mrs. Woodcock's, taken from her 'Experiences of an Officer's Wife
      in Ireland', p. 556. Hers is a fascinating account of life with an intelligence officer
      in 1920.

20   See Townshend, 'Bloody Sunday'.

21   See Townshend, *British Campaign*, pp. 173–196; Hart, *IRA and Its Enemies*, pp.
      93–108. Regarding the latter, however, see also Joost Augusteijn, *From Public Defi-
      ance to Guerrilla Warfare*, pp. 244–5. In Cork, IRA intelligence did score a major
      victory by tapping into military telegraph traffic, but not, apparently, until after
      the Truce.

22   On improving British efforts, see Eunan O'Halpin, 'Collins and Intelligence', pp.
      72–4 and Townshend, *British Campaign*, pp. 175–6, 195.

23   See Maj.-Gen. Sir Kenneth Strong, *Intelligence at the Top*, pp. 1–5.

24   O'Halpin, *Decline of the Union*, pp. 159–61.

25   Hart, *IRA and Its Enemies*, pp. 293–315.

26   Bew, 'Moderate Nationalism and the Irish Revolution', pp. 741–6.

27   See Thomas Mockaitis, *British Counterinsurgency, 1919–60*.

Notes to Narrative

1   Five 'G'· Division detectives had been shot in 1919.

2   The 5th and 6th Divisions were created as part of a general territorial
     reorganization of the British army in Nov. 1919. The latter, commanded by Maj.-
     Gen. Peter Strickland, covered Munster and south Leinster, with its headquarters
     in Cork city. Dublin District was created as a separate divisional command in
     January 1920 under Maj.-Gen. Gerald Boyd. Its area grew over time, as described
     later in the report.

3   Headquartered at the Curragh, County Kildare under Maj.-Gen. Hugh Jeudwine,

the 5th Division originally covered the whole of Ireland outside Dublin District and the 6th Division, including nearly the whole of Connaught and Ulster.

4   In contemporary military terms I(a) duties concerned operational intelligence such as the enemy's location and order of battle. I(b) dealt with secret service intelligence, such as that gathered in enemy-occupied territory.

5   Maj.-Gen. Sir Nevil Macready (1862–1946), formerly Adjutant-General and Commissioner of the Metropolitan Police, was appointed General Officer Commanding-in-Chief of Irish Command in March 1920.

6   For the context of this quotation see chp. VII of the Winter narrative following.

7   Brig.-Gen. Cuthbert Lucas (1879–1958), GOC 16th Infantry Brigade, was kidnapped by the IRA while fishing in north Cork in June 1920. He escaped a month later.

8   Terence MacSwiney, Lord Mayor of Cork and commander, 1st Cork Brigade from Mar. 1920. There is no evidence that his hunger strike was anything but genuine, although this was a common suspicion. Other men lasted even longer than he did.

9   A popular term for Irish outlaws of the late seventeenth and eighteenth centuries.

10   On 21 November 1920—'Bloody Sunday'—the Dublin IRA killed fourteen men and wounded others, many of whom were connected with the British intelligence effort. In retaliation, Auxiliary cadets killed twelve people at a gaelic football match and later killed two captured IRA officers and a third man 'while trying to escape' from Dublin Castle.

11   Field-Marshal Lord John French (1852–1925), formerly Commander-in-Chief, Home Forces, was Lord Lieutenant of Ireland from May 1918 to April 1921. From April 1920 the Chief Secretary of Ireland was Hamar Greenwood (1870–1948).

12   In March 1920 the RIC was divided—as it had been in the previous century—into four provincial divisions, with an additional one in Dublin. Each was commanded by a Divisional Commissioner.

13   Basil Thomson (1861–1939), Assistant Commissioner, Metropolitan Police, 1913–19; Home Office Director of Intelligence, 1919–21.

14   General Strickland, the GOC in the martial law area, was also its Military Governor.

15   Dublin Castle, the seat of Irish government.

16   The 5th Battalion of the Dublin Brigade, IRA was made up of 'engineers' whose main job was making weapons.

17   British information was wrong: there was no such position as Commander-in-Chief of the IRA.

18   Eamon de Valera (1882–1975) was President of Sinn Féin and Dáil Éireann.

19   Arthur Griffith (1871–1922), Vice-President of Sinn Féin; acting President of Dáil Éireann, June 1919–Nov. 1920.

20　Michael Collins (1890–1922) officially became the IRA's Director of Intelligence (or 'Information') in 1919, while holding the posts of Director of Organization and Adjutant-General. He was also Minister of Finance in the Dáil government and President of the Supreme Council of the Irish Republican Brotherhood.

21　Eamonn Duggan (1874–1936), was Director of Intelligence for part of 1920 until his arrest.

22　The London headquarters of the Home Office Directorate of Intelligence.

23　These six members of the IRA were killed by British soldiers at Clogheen, just outside Cork city.

24　Ernie O'Malley (1898–1957) was an organizer for IRA headquarters (GHQ) from 1918 and was appointed commander of the 2nd Southern Division in April 1921.

25　June was probably the worst month for the city guerrillas but, while hard-pressed and low on ammunition, they did not cease their attacks on soldiers, policemen and informers.

26　In fact, the IRA did have regular access to police codes. The cypher referred to was found on Terence MacSwiney, precipitating his conviction and hunger strike.

27　The man's name was David Walsh. His case is recounted in more detail in chap. VI of the Winter narrative.

28　In *The IRA and Its Enemies* (pp. 293–315) I argue that the great majority of those shot as informers in Cork were not British agents, and that many actual informers were spared because they were protected by their social position and connections. Some condemned West Cork Protestants did give, or try to give, information but there is no evidence that they acted *en masse* despite this statement. It is worth quoting Major Percival, the 'exceptionally experienced' officer mentioned, on 'the Protestant element': 'a few, but not many, were brave enough to assist the Crown Forces with information.'

29　This episode took place on 27 June, 1921, at Waterfall, County Cork, much as described. However, the 39 men arrested were not all IRA officers and Walter Leo Murphy, the local battalion commander, was shot as he ran from the pub. Another arrested man, Charlie Daly, was killed 'attempting to escape' the next day.

30　Winter's frequent comments on Irish society and character were by no means untypical of British officers or officials. Such attitudes, however common and however much products of their time, cannot have helped in the intelligent assessment of Irish revolutionaries.

31　Augustine Birrell (1850–1933), Chief Secretary of Ireland, 1907–1916.

32　The Vice-Regal Commission on the Re-Organization and Pay of the Irish Police Forces. The resulting Constabulary and Police (Ireland) Bill became law in Nov. 1919.

33   Eunan O'Halpin, however, blames 'a lack of initiative, rather than a shortage of cash' for police failure: 'British Intelligence in Ireland', p. 56.

34   James Carey (1845–83), a republican revolutionary turned informer whose evidence led to the conviction of five of those involved in the 1882 Phoenix Park murders. He was killed on this account.

35   Alan Bell (1857–1920), a longtime resident magistrate and former RIC officer, was appointed to a secret committee on intelligence in Nov. 1919. He was pursuing several investigations when he was shot dead in Dublin in March 1920.

36   Dan Breen (1894–1969) was a volunteer of the South Tipperary Brigade, famous—and wanted by the police—for his involvement in the Soloheadbeg ambush in Jan. 1919 and subsequent affrays.

37   I know of no such executions of volunteers for desertion or the like.

38   The Cliffony (Co. Sligo) ambush took place on 25 Oct. 1921. Three policemen were killed and another wounded.

39   Linda Kearns (b.1888), a veteran of the 1916 Rising, was arrested in April 1921.

40   Louis Darcy, commander of the Headford Battalion, IRA, was arrested and killed 'while trying to escape' in March 1921.

41   The action at Tourmakeady, Co. Mayo, took place on 3 May 1921. The initial ambush killed four policemen and the subsequent pursuit of the attackers by the British army killed one IRA officer and wounded another. The guerrillas succeeded in escaping capture and there is no evidence that an informer played any part in the event.

42   This was a Major C. A. Cameron, an old friend of Winter's and a fellow artilleryman, who had been on secret service in Holland during the war. Winter, *Winter's Tale*, pp. 220–1.

43   'F. Digby Hardy' was an alias; the man's real name is unknown.

44   Mary Lindsay of Coachford, Co. Cork—a widow—was kidnapped and executed as an informer by the IRA in 1921, against the wishes of the GHQ.

45   Vincent Fovargue was killed on 3 April, 1921.

46   Tom Hales, the commander of the West Cork Brigade, was tortured after his arrest in July 1920, despite British claims to the contrary. There is no corroborating evidence that he gave any information to his captors.

47   Richard Mulcahy (1886–1971) was the IRA's Chief of Staff from March 1918.

48   O'Malley was not present on this occasion, 28 Nov. 1920. Better known as the Kilmichael ambush, this saw a West Cork flying column led by Tom Barry wipe out an Auxiliary patrol.

49   Father Dominic, OFM Capuchin, was the chaplain of the 1st Cork Brigade. He upheld the morality of the guerrilla campaign against the Bishop of Cork's decree of excommunication in December 1920. He was later transferred to the USA by his superiors.

50   This was known to the IRA as the 'murder gang' or the 'Igoe gang' after its sup-
     posed commander.

51   P.J. Lynch edited the *Weekly Independent* and the *Sunday Independent* from 1905.
     The *Independent*'s London correspondent was also accused of being an agent for
     Michael Collins—an accusation the paper denied but which may well have been
     true. I am grateful to Patrick Maume for this information.

52   District Inspector Percival Lee-Wilson (1887–1920) was shot in Gorey, Co.
     Wexford on 15 June 1920. As an officer in the Royal Irish Regiment he had been
     accused of mistreating prisoners after the Easter Rising in Dublin.

53   Rear-Admiral Hugh 'Quex' Sinclair (1873–1939), Director of Naval Intelligence,
     1919–21 and later head of the Secret Intelligence Service.

54   Eileen MacGrane, a lecturer at the National University, was on the executive of
     Cumann na mBan and was the first woman to be court-martialled since 1916.
     Michael Collins used her home in Dublin as one of his offices. She spent several
     months in prison.

55   Gearoid O'Sullivan (1881–1948) replaced Michael Collins as Adjutant-General
     of the IRA in February 1920.

56   Patricia Hoey, a journalist, was not Michael Collins's secretary. He did use her
     home as an office, for which she was arrested and jailed in 1921.

57   Erskine Childers (1870–1922) was appointed Director of Publicity for Dail Eir-
     eann in March 1921.

58   The report was written by the O/C, 3rd Battalion, 1st Cork Brigade. It was this
     failed ambush that led to the death of Mrs. Lindsay.

59   On 20 February 1921 an IRA column was trapped and nearly wiped out near
     Clonmult, Co. Cork.

60   Desmond FitzGerald (1888–1947) was Director of Publicity for Dáil Éireann
     from 1919 until his arrest in March 1921.

61   Cathal Brugha (1874–1922)—born Charles Burgess—was Minister of Defence
     in the Dáil government from 1919. He vehemently opposed the Anglo-Irish
     Treaty.

62   Lt. Col. John Carter (1882–1944), Imperial General Staff officer (MI5); Metro-
     politan Police, 1919; Deputy Assistant Commissioner, 1922 (replacing Basil
     Thomson).

Bibliography

Andrew, Christopher, *Secret Service: The Making of the British Intelligence Community* (London, 1985)

Augusteijn, Joost, *From Public Defiance to Guerrilla Warfare* (Dublin, 1996)

Bew, Paul, 'Moderate Nationalism and the Irish Revolution, 1916–1923', *Historical Journal*, vol. xlii (1999), pp. 729–49

Coogan, Tim Pat, *Michael Collins: A Biography* (London, 1990)

Duggan, G.C., ('Periscope'), 'The Last Days of Dublin Castle', *Blackwood's Magazine*, ccxii, no. 1,282 (1922), pp. 137–90

Gudgin, Peter, *Military Intelligence: The British Story* (London, 1989)

Hart, Peter, *The IRA and Its Enemies: Violence and Community in Cork, 1916–1923* (Oxford, 1998)

Jeffery, Keith, 'British Military Intelligence Following World War I', in K.G. Robertson (ed.), *British and American Approaches to Intelligence* (London, 1987), pp. 55–83

MacDonagh, O. (ed.), *Ireland and Irish-Australia: Studies in Cultural and Political History* (London, 1988), pp. 175–194

Macready, General Sir Nevil, *Annals of an Active Life* (London, 1924)

Mandle, W.F., 'Sir Antony MacDonnell and Crime Branch Special', in Mandle and Oliver

Mockaitis, Thomas R., *British Counterinsurgency, 1919–60* (London, 1990)

Neligan, David, *The Spy in the Castle* (London, 1968)

Novick, Ben, 'Postal Censorship in Ireland, 1914–16', *Irish Historical Studies*, xxxi, no. 123 (1999)

O'Halpin, Eunan, 'British Intelligence in Ireland, 1914–1921', in Christopher Andrew and David Dilks (eds.), *The Missing Dimension: Governments and Intelligence Communities in the Twentieth Century* (London, 1984), pp. 54–77

——. *The Decline of the Union: British Government in Ireland 1892–1920* (Dublin, 1987)

——. 'Collins and Intelligence', in Gabriel Doherty and Dermot Keogh (eds.), *Michael Collins and the Making of the Irish State* (Cork, 1998), pp. 68–80

Strong, Sir Kenneth, *Intelligence at the Top* (London, 1968)

Townshend, Charles, *The British Campaign in Ireland 1919–1921: The Development of Political and Military Policies* (Oxford, 1975)

——. 'Bloody Sunday – Michael Collins Speaks', *European Studies Review*, ix, no. 3 (1979), pp. 377–85

——. 'The Irish Republican Army and the Development of Guerrilla Warfare, 1916–1921' *English Historical Review*, xciv, no. 371 (1979), pp. 318–45

Winter, Sir Ormonde, *Winter's Tale: An Autobiography* (London, 1955)

Woodcock, Mrs., 'Experiences of an Officer's Wife in Ireland', *Blackwood's Magazine*, ccxi, no. 1,267 (1921), pp. 553–96

Index